Cambridge Elements

Elements in Religion and Monotheism
edited by
Paul K. Moser
Loyola University Chicago
Chad Meister
Affiliate Scholar, Ansari Institute for Global Engagement with Religion, University of Notre Dame

MONOTHEISM AND RELIGIOUS EXPERIENCE

Mark Owen Webb
Texas Tech University

Shaftesbury Road, Cambridge CB2 8EA, United Kingdom

One Liberty Plaza, 20th Floor, New York, NY 10006, USA

477 Williamstown Road, Port Melbourne, VIC 3207, Australia

314–321, 3rd Floor, Plot 3, Splendor Forum, Jasola District Centre, New Delhi – 110025, India

103 Penang Road, #05–06/07, Visioncrest Commercial, Singapore 238467

Cambridge University Press is part of Cambridge University Press & Assessment, a department of the University of Cambridge.

We share the University's mission to contribute to society through the pursuit of education, learning and research at the highest international levels of excellence.

www.cambridge.org
Information on this title: www.cambridge.org/9781009547772

DOI: 10.1017/9781108955317

When citing this work, please include a reference to the DOI 10.1017/9781108955317

First published 2024

A catalogue record for this publication is available from the British Library

ISBN 978-1-009-54777-2 Hardback
ISBN 978-1-108-95802-8 Paperback
ISSN 2631-3014 (online)
ISSN 2631-3006 (print)

Monotheism and Religious Experience

Elements in Religion and Monotheism

DOI: 10.1017/9781108955317
First published online: December 2024

Mark Owen Webb
Texas Tech University

Author for correspondence: Mark Owen Webb, Mark.Webb@ttu.edu

Abstract: In the monotheistic traditions, there are people who report having special experiences that justify their monotheistic beliefs. They see, hear, or otherwise experience directly the one true God, ruler of the universe. In order to understand what is going on in these experiences and how we should respond to reports of these experiences, it is important to understand what religious experiences can and can't be, what the claim of monotheism entails, and therefore how what reports of such experiences mean, both for the experiencer and for the recipient of the report.

Keywords: monotheism, religious experience, mysticism, God, religions

ISBNs: 9781009547772 (HB), 9781108958028 (PB), 9781108955317 (OC)
ISSNs: 2631-3014 (online), 2631-3006 (print)

Contents

Preface

This work comes late in a career dominated by the topic of religious experience. From my first days an undergraduate at Texas Tech University, I have been in turns fascinated, frustrated, and possessed by a desire to understand what is going on in religious experiences and what they mean. My first publication, my dissertation, and my first book were on the topic. As a result, a large number of people over the last forty-odd years have contributed to my understanding, far too many to acknowledge in a short preface. Obviously, my work owes a deep debt to the late William P. Alston, my dissertation director and inspiration, both as a philosopher and as a human being. I also owe gratitude to the students in my Spring 2024 seminar in the Philosophy of Religion for input on Section 2 and to my wife, Virginia Downs, for various contributions throughout.

The central aim of this work is to examine the idea of religious experience in the context of the monotheistic religious traditions, for all of which it seems to play an important role. This examination involves two closely related concerns. First, does it make sense to speak of an experience of God as conceived by those religions? That is, can a being of that kind, infinitely beyond our ordinary experience and completely different from the physical universe, be the object of a human experience? Second, if it is possible for human beings to experience such a being, can those experiences play an evidential role in religious beliefs? That is, can such experiences ever be good reason for religious belief? I hope to show that the answer to both questions is "Yes," and that various prima facie problems for thinking so can be answered using only the resources of the religions in question.

Section 1 is a minor reworking of my Stanford Encyclopedia of Philosophy article on religious experience and Section 2 is a minor reworking of my essay "Meaning and Value in Religious Experience," which appeared in the *Cambridge Companion to Religious Experience*, Paul Moser and Chad Meister, eds., New York: Cambridge University Press, 2020.

1 Religious Experience

There is a certain strain in Christian theology and apologetics according to which the existence of God and the major truths of religion can be established by argument, evidence, and good old-fashioned proof.[1] There

[1] For example, Saint Thomas Aquinas, Saint Anselm, Moses Maimonides, and Ibn Rushd are paradigms of the idea in the medieval period. The project has continued until the present day, with such figures as Richard Swinburne and William Craig.

are similar strains of Islamic and Jewish theology. There is another strain in Christian theology according to which knowledge of God is an internal matter, attributable to an inner witness, illumination of the spirit, or the like. Both strains of thought are present from the beginnings of the religious traditions they address. Thinkers in the first group are often suspicious of the claims of thinkers in the second group. How, they ask, can the objective reality of *anything* be known by inward feelings? "I just feel it is true" has never been a good answer to a question of why a person believes a thing.

There is a hymn sung in many evangelical churches called "He Lives"; it contains the line, "You ask me how I know he lives; he lives within my heart."[2] A teacher of a course called "Christian Evidences" in Lubbock, Texas was locally famous for scoffing at that line. He would hold his hand over his heart and simper, saying, "I feel it in my heart," remarking that such a claim made the assertion both unanswerable and unverifiable. He wrote, "God has never left it for people to learn of gospel truths by subjective interpretations of their personal experience."[3] Instead, he thought, we can – and must – rely on objective facts to prove that the New Testament speaks the truth, and so we can *know* Jesus lives. Not only can we know it, we can prove it to others. He has a point, at least about subjective experiences. One need only look at the human history of psychics, fortune tellers, proponents of the alleged "law of attraction,"[4] and others who speak with assurance (and presumably some are sincere) about what is true but turn out to be wrong. Even in the cases when we don't have any way to tell whether they are right or wrong, instances in which the deliverances of one person's feelings contradict the deliverances of someone else's feelings are legion. It is a pervasively unreliable method of forming beliefs. There is serious danger in relying on inner feelings for guidance on important topics.

It is tempting to think that most people know wishful thinking is a terrible way to form beliefs, but even the sensible among us are prone to being misled by our feelings. The problem is heightened when we realize how prone we are to pareidolia, self-deception, and motivated reasoning.[5] Pareidolia is the human

[2] This is a popular hymn written by Alfred Henry Ackley in 1933, and can be found in almost every Protestant hymnal.

[3] Edward C. Wharton, *Christianity: A Clear Case of History*, West Monroe: Howard, 1977, p. 201. Ed. Wharton was known to his students as "Doctor Know."

[4] Famously promoted by books like *The Secret*, by Rhonda Byrne, which is still dismayingly popular.

[5] These various psychological phenomena are often used in Cognitive Science of Religion as a naturalistic explanation of religious experience and the arising of religious belief. See Justin L. Barrett, "Exploring the Natural Foundations of Religion." *Trends in Cognitive Sciences* 4,

tendency to perceive patterns in random data and so contributes to false attributions of agency. This is most clearly illustrated by the phenomenon of seeing Mary or some other figure in the grain of a piece of wood and thinking that appearance was miraculously produced. A prudent person doesn't trust such things, even in him or herself. The possibility of illusion, delusion, or hallucination can never just be dismissed. As the prophet Jeremiah lamented, "The heart is more deceitful than all else and is desperately sick; Who can understand it?"[6]

It seems that, for reasons like these, we should dismiss people's claims of having encountered God. But this conclusion is in tension with another mundane fact about the human epistemic condition: In most instances, human beings rightly treat other human beings as excellent sources of information. When someone tells us what they saw or heard, we generally believe them, and rightly so. We wouldn't get very far in acquiring knowledge if we relied on only what we can gather with our own built-in equipment. Fortunately, most people tell the truth, so we can pool our knowledge, and thus each of us has access to a vast amount of information. Of course, there are people who abuse the trust we extend them and lie to us. There are innocent mistakes, too. These are situations in which the other person's report is not so helpful. Fortunately, through long experience, we have developed techniques for sniffing out the unreliable claims. We apply rules of thumb, which highlight situations in which someone is likely to lie (generally, they have something to gain from your believing them, whether what they say is true or not) or likely to be mistaken (they don't have the kind of expertise they would need, their eyesight is not so good, what they say contradicts something else we have excellent reason to believe, etc.). It is not a perfect system by any means. Not only does it not catch all the insincere or unreliable people, it also will falsely eliminate some sincere and competent people, whom we should believe. Nevertheless, these caveats help us make better decisions about whom to believe and whom to dismiss.[7]

The amount of credence we should extend to a person's claims can vary not only with how sincere and competent the person is, by also by what the content of the claim is. Some categories of claim are clearly unproblematic (though in a particular case there may be reason for skepticism): what our parents tell us when we are children; what scientists speaking in their area of expertise say;

(2000), 29–34 and Pascal Boyer. *Religion Explained: The Evolutionary Origins of Religious Thought*, New York: Basic Books, 2001.

6 Jeremiah 17:9, New American Standard translation.

7 For examinations of why (and under what conditions) we should trust one another, see Axel Gelfert, *A Critical Introduction to Testimony*, New York: Bloomsbury Academic, 2014; and Cecil A. J. Coady, *Testimony: A Philosophical Study*, New York: Clarendon Press, 1992.

what people report about their own lives and experiences, and the like, to give just a few examples. Likewise, some categories of claims are problematic (though in a particular case there may be reason to be less skeptical): a salesperson's claim about the condition of what he wants to sell you; the claims of a person known to you to be a habitual liar; an untrained layperson making claims that contradict what the scientists say, and the like, for example. We tend to agree about which categories of claims deserve more scrutiny and which do not.

An interesting problem arises when there is a category of claim some say is problematic, and some say is not. This is the case with the category of claim I am discussing in this Element: claims about religious experiences. Some say, for a variety of reasons, that they are simply illusory, like hallucinations, so we should group them with other claims made by unreliable people, or people using unreliable means and methods. Others say they are experiences, like any other, and so we should accept the claims, just as we generally accept people's reports of what they saw, heard, etc. Still others say whether they are real experiences or not, we should withhold belief from all of them, as there seems to be no way to settle who is right. There are good, principled reasons in favor of all of these responses.

The idea of religious experience captures the imagination in a way no other theological idea does. The thought that God (or a god, or a saint, or an angel) might choose to reveal himself to me, a mere mortal, is exciting. It is the prospect of an ordinary life turning into a world-changing, special life. This is part of the reason we find the stories of Abraham, Moses, Muhammad, and many others so compelling. The Buddha is a transcendental figure not because he teaches a life transforming truth, but because he discovered it, came face to face with it, in his own inner quest. The thought that a mortal can "pull back the curtain" and experience the basic realities is intriguing and exciting. This Element is about what it means to pull that curtain back and find, behind it all, a single God.

1.1 Delineation of the Topic

Before we get anywhere, we will need be clear on what kinds of experiences count, and what kind don't.[8] We need to distinguish religious experiences properly so called from various nearby phenomena. First of all, we want to distinguish religious experience from objectless feelings. It is tempting to call

[8] The following two sections are taken from my article, "Religious Experience," *The Stanford Encyclopedia of Philosophy* (Fall Ed.), Edward N. Zalta & Uri Nodelman (eds.), 2022, https://plato.stanford.edu/archives/fall2022/entries/religious-experience/.

feelings of elation religious experiences, especially when they are brought on in religious settings. Two important recent theorists of religion, Rudolf Otto and Friedrich Schleiermacher, began their inquiries into the nature of religion with examinations of religious feelings. For Schleiermacher, the essence of religious experience is the "feeling of absolute dependence."[9] He identified as the essential feature of religious experiences that they take us out of ourselves. They decenter us with the intense awareness that we are not our own makers, that we depend for our very being on something other than ourselves. Otto extends this account by isolating particular features of those feelings, including features that attribute properties to the cause of the feelings, which he calls the "numinous." In order to distinguish the feeling from other kinds of feelings of helplessness, powerlessness, or smallness, he identifies the special feeling of encounters with the numinous as "creature feeling." The idea is that it is not mere dependence, but the feeling of being "submerged and overwhelmed ... in contrast to that which is supreme above all creatures."[10] While Schleiermacher and Otto offer a penetrating phenomenology of what we may call religious experience, they still give an account only of the feelings involved; what is missing is the idea of experience as a relation to something other than my own feelings. What are we adding to the story when we add to the analysis of the feeling an account of a cause of that feeling that is objectively real and outside of me?

Another kind of experience often called religious experience is the experience of something ordinary, but as having special religious significance. An aspect of the natural world, like the sea, or the starry sky, can often come to a person with the conviction that there is a creator behind it. The photographer Thomas Oord describes the experience eloquently:

> Several years ago, I felt God's presence while photographing in the Owyhee Mountains of Idaho. A beautiful cloud formed one evening, and the setting sun painted its underbelly an array of colors. As the sky-canvas developed, I ran about positioning my camera and making photos. The beauty prompted me to "get on my Pentecostal." I repeatedly shouted "Hallelujah!"

In monotheistic traditions, it is thought that we can learn about God through the book of scripture and also through the book of nature. As Saint Paul says to the Romans, "For since the creation of the world His invisible attributes, His eternal power and divine nature, have been clearly seen, being understood through what has been made, so that they are without excuse."[11] The same thought is expressed

[9] Friedrich Schleiermacher, *On Religion: Speeches to Its Cultured Despisers*, Richard Crouter (trans. & ed.), Cambridge: Cambridge University Press, 1988.

[10] Rudoph Otto, *The Idea of the Holy*, New York: Oxford, 1950, p. 10.

[11] Romans 1:20, New American Standard translation.

in the Psalm, "The heavens are telling of the glory of God; And their expanse is declaring the work of His hands . . . "[12] And in the Qur'an:

> Behold! in the creation of the heavens and the earth; in the alternation of the night and the day; in the sailing of the ships through the ocean for the profit of mankind; in the rain which Allah Sends down from the skies, and the life which He gives therewith to an earth that is dead; in the beasts of all kinds that He scatters through the earth; in the change of the winds, and the clouds which they Trail like their slaves between the sky and the earth;- (Here) indeed are Signs for a people that are wise.[13]

As significant as such experiences can be, they complicate the picture by adding ordinary sense-experience to the mix. While it is certainly reasonable to count such experiences as religious experiences, to know what is essential to religious experiences, we should set those aside. For this purpose, religious experiences can be characterized generally as experiences that seem to the person having them to be of some objective reality not accessible to the physical senses, of some being more important than the person, and to have some religious import.

1.2 Typologies

Reports of religious experiences reveal a variety of different kinds. Many are visual or auditory presentations (visions and auditions), but not through the physical eyes or ears. Subjects report "seeing" or "hearing," but quickly disavow any claim to seeing or hearing with bodily sense organs. Such experiences are easy to dismiss as hallucinations, but the subjects of the experience frequently claim that though it is entirely internal, such as a hallucination or imagination, it is nevertheless a veridical experience, through some spiritual analog of the eye or ear (William James and Alston cite many examples).[14] In other cases, the language of "seeing" is used in its extended sense of realization, as when a yogi is said to "see" his or her identity with Brahman; Buddhists speak of "seeing things as they are" as one of the hallmarks of true enlightenment, where this means grasping or realizing the emptiness of things, but not in a purely intellectual way.

Another type is the religious experience that comes through sensory experiences of ordinary objects, but seems to carry with it extra information about some supramundane reality. Examples include experiencing God in nature, in the starry sky, or a flower, or the like. A second person standing nearby would

12 Psalm 19:1, New American Standard translation.

13 *Al-Baqara* 2:64, A. Yusuf Ali translation.

14 William James, *The Varieties of Religious Experience: A Study in Human Nature Being the Gifford Lectures on Natural Religion Delivered at Edinburgh in 1901–1902*, New York: Longmans, Green, 1917; William Alston, *Perceiving God: The Epistemology of Religious Experience*, Ithaca: Cornell University Press, 1991.

see exactly the same sky or flower but would not necessarily have the further religious content to his or her experience. There are also cases in which the religious experience just is an ordinary perception, but the physical object is itself the object of religious significance. Moses's experience of the burning bush, or the Buddha's disciples watching him levitate, are examples of this type. A second person standing nearby would see exactly the same phenomenon. Witnesses to miracles are having that kind of religious experience, whether they understand it that way or not.[15] Another subtype of this type has been suggested by Ekstrom.[16] She argues that suffering could be a kind of religious experience, not because the objects of your experience are of the relevant type, but rather because your experience is from the point of view of the suffering Christ, and so shares in his experience. You vicariously experience the world from Christ's point of view. It is reasonable to think that part of the content of an experience is the subject's point of view, that experiencing Christ's suffering is, at least in part, experiencing Christ himself, whether you recognize it as such or not.

A fourth type of religious experience is harder to describe: it can't be characterized accurately in sensory language, even analogically, yet the subject of the experience insists that the experience is a real, direct awareness of some religiously significant reality external to the subject. These kinds of experiences are usually described as "ineffable."

As long as we think of religious experiences as purportedly real contact with an object of religious significance, we also have to leave open the logical possibility that people could be in some kind of experiential contact with such a being without being aware of it. It is not at all unusual for an object to enter one's visual field, and information about it is received and processed by the brain, but the subject has no conscious awareness of the object. Just as in the case of nonepistemic seeing[17] there might be nonepistemic religious experience. That is, a person could have an experience that is in fact an experience of God without experiencing him *as* God.[18] Eleonore Stump makes a persuasive case:

---

[15] This fact leaves open the possibility that one might have a religious experience of any of these kinds, but not recognize it as such. The possibility of so-called "*de re*" religious experiences is intriguing, and anyone who believes in *de re* thoughts or beliefs should leave that possibility open, it is obvious that they can't enter into the justification of fires-person religious belief.

[16] Laura W. Ekstrom, "Suffering as Religious Experience," in Peter Van Inwagen (ed.), *Christian Faith and the Problem of Evil*, Grand Rapids: Eerdmans Press, 2004, pp. 95–110.

[17] This idea is nicely explained by Fred Dretske in his 1969 book, *Seeing and Knowing*, Chicago: The University of Chicago Press.

[18] William Wainwright explores the possibility of these kinds of experiences as possibly sufficient for soteriological purposes in William J. Wainwright, "Jonathan Edwards and the Hiddenness of God," in Daniel Howard-Snyder & Paul K. Moser (eds.), *Divine Hiddenness: New Essays*, Cambridge University Press, 2002, pp. 98–119.

> [I]t seems to me that it is possible to receive something of the consolation of God's presence and love without recognizing it as such. The consolation of love, and its opposites, need not operate at the level of full consciousness. We know now that even those rendered unconscious by anesthetics apprehend comments made by their surgeons and nurses, so that healing is hindered by crude or demeaning conversation on the part of medical personnel during the course of an operation. Analogously, a person sufficiently sick might not know that her daughter was with her; but, somewhat below the level of her consciousness, her daughter's presence might nonetheless produce psychic ease and peace. In the same way, perhaps it is possible even for a person who believes of himself that he is alienated from God, or that he is an atheist, to receive some kind of consolation from God's presence, provided that, contrary to what he believes of himself, he has not closed God out entirely.[19]

Though this kind of experience is no help in providing epistemological foundations for religious belief, it is nevertheless a possible kind that our account should include.

Depending on one's purposes, other ways of dividing up religious experiences will suggest themselves. For example, William James[20] divides experiences into "healthy-minded" and "sick-minded," according to the personality of the subject, which colors the content of the experience itself. Keith Yandell[21] divides them into five categories, according to the content of the experiences: monotheistic, nirvanic (enlightenment experiences associated with Buddhism), kevalic (enlightenment experiences associated with Jainism), moksha (experiences of release from karma, associated with Hinduism), and nature experiences. Differences of object certainly make differences in content, and so make differences in what can be said about the experiences.

While in the monotheistic traditions, religious experiences are treated as experiences of the one true god, in other traditions, it is not necessarily a personal being who is the object of the experience, or even a positive being at all. In the traditions that find their origin in the Indian subcontinent – chiefly Hinduism, Buddhism, and Jainism – the object of religious experiences is some basic fact or feature of reality, rather than some entity separate from the universe. In the orthodox Hindu traditions, one may certainly have an experience of a god or some other supernatural entity (like Arjuna's encounter with Krishna in the Bhagavad Gita), but a great many important kinds of experiences are of Brahman, and its identity with the self. In Yoga, which is based in the Samkhya understanding of the nature of

[19] Eleonore Stump, *Wandering in Darkness: Narrative and the Problem of Suffering*, New York: Oxford University Press, 2010, p. 623, note 112.

[20] William James, *The Varieties of Religious Experience: A Study in Human Nature Being the Gifford Lectures on Natural Religion Delivered at Edinburgh in 1901–1902.*

[21] Keith Yandell, *Epistemology of Religious Experience*, Cambridge: Cambridge University Press, 1993.

things, the mystical practice of yoga leads to a calming and stilling of the mind, which allows the yogi to apprehend directly that he or she is not identical to, or even causally connected with, the physical body, and this realization is what liberates him or her from suffering.

In Theravada Buddhism, the goal of meditation is to "see things as they are," which is to see them as unsatisfactory, impermanent, and not-self.[22] The meditator, as he or she makes progress along the way, sheds various delusions and attachments. The last one to go is the delusion that he or she is a self. To see this is to see all of reality as made up of sequences of momentary events, each causally dependent on the ones that went before. There are no abiding substances, and no eternal souls. Seeing reality that way extinguishes the fires of craving and liberates the meditator from the necessity of rebirth.[23] Seeing things as they are involves removing from the mind all the delusions that stand in the way of such seeing, which is done by meditation practices that develop the meditator's mastery of his or her own mind. The type of meditation that brings this mastery and allows the meditator to see the true nature of things is called *Vipassana* (insight) meditation. It typically involves some object of meditation, which can be some feature of the meditator him- or herself, some feature of the physical or mental world, or some abstraction, which then becomes the focus of the meditator's concentration and examination. In the end, it is hoped, the meditator will see in the object the unsatisfactory and impermanent nature of things and that there is no self to be found in them. At the moment of that insight, *nirvana* is achieved. While the experience of nirvana is essentially the realization of a kind of insight, it is also accompanied by other experiential elements, especially of the cessation of negative mental states. Nirvana is described in the Buddhist canon as the extinction of the fires of desire. The Theravada tradition teaches other kinds of meditation that can help the meditator make progress, but the final goal can't be achieved without *vipassana* meditation.

In the Mahayana Buddhist traditions, this idea of the constantly fluctuating nature of the universe is extended in various ways. For some, even those momentary events that make up the flow of the world are understood to be empty of inherent existence (the idea of inherent existence is understood differently in different traditions) to the point that what one sees in the enlightenment experience is the ultimate emptiness (*sunyata*) of all things. In the Yogacara school of Mahayana Buddhism, this is understood as emptiness of external existence; that is, to see things as they are is to see them as all mind-dependent. In the Zen school of Mahayana Buddhism, the enlightenment

[22] Christopher Gowans, *Philosophy of the Buddha*, New York: Routledge, 2003, p. 191.

[23] Stephen Laumakis, *An Introduction to Buddhist Philosophy*, Cambridge: Cambridge University Press, 2008, pp. 158–161.

experience (*kensho*) reveals that reality contains no distinctions or dualities. Since concepts and language always involve distinctions, which always involve duality, the insight so gained cannot be achieved conceptually or expressed linguistically. In all Mahayana schools, what brings enlightenment is direct realization of *sunyata* as a basic fact about reality.

The situation is somewhat more complicated in the Chinese traditions. The idea of religious experience seems to be almost completely absent in the Confucian tradition; the social world looms large, and the idea of an ultimate reality that needs to be experienced becomes much less prominent. Before the arrival of Buddhism in China, Confucianism was primarily a political and ethical system, with no particular concern with the transcendent (though people who identified themselves as Confucians frequently engaged in Chinese folk religious practices). Nevertheless, meditation (and therefore something that could be called "religious experience") did come to play a role in Confucian practice in the tenth century, as Confucian thought began to be influenced by Buddhist and Daoist thought. The resulting view is known as Neo-Confucianism. Neo-Confucianism retains the Mencian doctrine that human beings are by nature good, but in need of purification. Since goodness resides in every person, then examination of oneself should reveal the nature of goodness, through the experience of the vital force within (*qi*). The form of meditation that arises from this line of thought ("quiet sitting" or "sitting and forgetting") is very like Buddhist vipassana meditation, but there is no value placed on any particular insight gained, though one can experience the principle of unity (*li*) behind the world. Success is measured in gradual moral improvement. The Daoist ideal is to come to an understanding of the Dao, the fundamental nature of reality that explains all things in the world, and live according to it. Knowledge of the Dao is essential to the good life, but this knowledge cannot be learned from discourses, or transmitted by teaching. It is only known by experiential acquaintance. The Dao gives the universe a kind of grain, or flow, going against which causes human difficulty. The good human life is then one that respects the flow of Dao, and goes along with it. This is what is meant by "life in accordance with nature." By paying attention, a person can learn what the Dao is, and can experience unity with it. This picture of reality, along with the picture of how one can come to know it, heavily influenced the development of Chan Buddhism, which became Zen.

Each of these kinds of religious experience are deserving of explicit treatment, and some have treated the general category, embracing all these different kinds.[24] Such a general treatment presents various difficulties, chief among which is the difficulty of finding a level of generality at which it makes sense to

24 John Hick 's *An Interpretation of Religion: Human Responses to the Transcendent*, 2nd. ed., New Haven: Yale University Press, 2004 is one heroic and notable attempt.

think of them as the same kind of thing. This difficulty is related to the problem of finding a level of generality at which all religions can be thought of as the same kind of thing, sometimes called the problem of defining the term *religion*.

Of course, we are not terribly concerned with defining a word (we're not writing a dictionary, after all), but rather describing the phenomenon of religion in a general way, analyzing the concept. There is a long history of people trying to do that very thing, and they tend to run into one or more of a small set of pitfalls. First, it is difficult to come up with a set of features that are necessary and sufficient to pick out all and only religions. Not all have gods, not all have scriptures, not all have an idea of life after death, and so on for all the obvious candidates. There seems to be no condition lack of which disqualifies a practice as a religion without admitting other kinds of human institutions and endeavors, like fandoms and political parties, that are certainly not religions. There seems to be no criterion that is either necessary or sufficient.

There is a way to secure an analysis that applies to all and only religions, but the cost is circularity. I could trivially say that a religion is a set of religious practices and call it a day. Such an analysis would be unhelpful. An account can be circular in more covert ways, too. If your account includes ideas like "supernatural," "divinity," "sacred," or any of a thousand other terms, that counts as covertly circular. To see why, consider the following attempted analysis: Religions are social institutions that offer their participants a relationship with the divine, and a hope of salvation. (It would be easy to quibble about whether this provides necessary and sufficient conditions, but let's leave that aside for now.) What counts as divine? When I talk to a being much more powerful than me and ask it to spare me from some terrible fate, what makes that a prayer to a divine being? What makes this being a divine being rather than just a natural but vastly superior one? What makes the favor I want from it salvation, rather than deliverance from some natural but mundane disaster? The answer seems to be that for the religious terms, the reference includes something supernatural, while the mundane ones include only natural phenomena. Religions necessarily involve something supernatural.

But what does "supernatural" mean? I presume we are not meant to take literally the idea of something above or beyond nature, in some special spatial relation to it. It is some kind of nonnatural thing. Something is nonnatural if it is real but cannot be accounted for by natural science. As straightforward as it is, such a story runs into the difficulty identified by Hempel in 1969.[25] We presumably don't mean science as we now know it, because we still have so much to learn. Something Physics can't account for today will be tomorrow's

[25] Carl Gustav Hempel, "Reduction: Ontological and Linguistic Facets," in S. Morgenbesser, P. Suppes & M. White (eds.), *Philosophy, Science, and Method: Essays in Honor of Ernest Nagel*, New York: St. Martin's Press, 1969, pp. 179–199.

commonplace in physics. Suppose we mean fully developed science when we have it all figured out. Do we really have any idea what such a science will be like? It seems that we have no clue whether, after science has reached its end, we will be able to fit ghosts and angels into the story, or even God.[26]

Fortunately, we can simplify that problem, first by limiting our discussion to one kind of purported experience, without either accounting for every kind of experience or providing a general definition of "religion." In general, we can distinguish between those experiences that treat the object of experience as part of or an aspect of oneself, those that treat the object of experience as an impersonal feature of the universe, and those that treat the object as a singular existent, separate from the experiencer him or herself. That last group includes those religious experiences that purport to be of a god or gods, as independently existing beings with their own wills, with whom the experiencer can interact. Among those are the experiences of what is designated "God"; that is, a one-of-a-kind, personal supreme being who holds some special authority over the experiencer. Religions that assert that there is exactly one such being are monotheistic religions, and religious experiences in those traditions are encounters with the one God. Those experiences are the topic of this work.

2 Monotheism

"Monotheism" is simple to define. It is simply the belief that there is exactly one God. As with most simple definitions, though, digging a little deeper reveals some hidden complexities. Monotheism contrasts with atheism on the one hand – the idea that there are no gods – and polytheism on the other – the idea that there is more than one god. Monotheism is easy to locate on this axis. But there is room in logical space for claims that there is exactly one of something that isn't exactly god. How to distinguish those nearby claims from monotheism depends on finding the boundaries of the concept of god (the lower-case "g" shows one place in logical space where problems can arise). When we call something a god, what are we saying about it?

2.1 What Is There Only One of?

In English-language philosophy of religion, it is commonplace to read that "God" *means* "the one and only omnipotent, omniscient, wholly good being,"[27] or at least

[26] I argue this in detail in "An Eliminativist Theory of Religion," *Sophia* 48 (2009), 35–42.

[27] See, for example William Wainwright's "Monotheism" article in the Stanford Encyclopedia of Philosophy. "Theists believe that reality's ultimate principle is God – an omnipotent, omniscient, goodness that is the creative ground of everything other than itself. Monotheism is the view that there is only one such God." Wainwright, William, "Monotheism," *The Stanford Encyclopedia of Philosophy* (Winter Ed.), Edward N. Zalta (ed.), 2021, https://plato.stanford.edu/archives/win2021/entries/monotheism/. Accessed 8/6/2023.

that God is necessarily maximally excellent in some way. For example (carefully avoiding talking about definitions) Richard Swinburne says

> By a theist I understand a man who believes that there is a God. By a "God" he understands something like a "person without a body (i.e. a spirit) who is eternal, free, able to do anything, knows everything, is perfectly good, is the proper object of human worship and obedience, the creator and sustainer of the universe."[28]

This idea is nicely summed up in Anselm's formula,

> Lord, do you, who do give understanding to faith, give me, so far as you knowest it to be profitable, to understand that you are as we believe; and that you are that which we believe. And indeed, we believe that you are a being than which nothing greater can be conceived.[29]

Aquinas defines "*deus*" as "that which exercises providence over all."[30] He says:

> For this name is imposed from His universal providence over all things; since all who speak of God intend to name God as exercising providence over all; hence Dionysius says (Div. Nom. ii), "The Deity watches over all with perfect providence and goodness."

There are disputes about whether the term is a proper name (or some other rigid designator) or an abbreviated definite description (or some other nonrigid descriptor),[31] but there is general agreement about qualities of the being so designated. For purposes of philosophical theology, surely there is nothing wrong with stipulating how you are going to use a word. Proving anything, especially existence, of any of these perfect beings is a significant enterprise.

From a historical point of view, this understanding of what "god" means is puzzling. First, we must recognize that the concept of god is, originally, the concept of something that need not be perfect, and need not be unique. When Moses told the Israelites that his people should have no other gods before him, the idea of a plurality of gods was natural. It was the idea that there is only one that was the innovation.[32] Some have suggested that Moses didn't actually give the

[28] Richard Swinburne, *Coherence of Theism*, Oxford University Press, Incorporated, 1977. *ProQuest Ebook Central*, https://ebookcentral.proquest.com/lib/ttu/detail.action?docID=3053289. Accessed 1/25/2023.

[29] Anselm *Proslogium* cha. 8.

[30] *Summa Theologiiae* Part I, Q 13, A 8.

[31] Alvin Plantinga, *Warranted Christian Belief*, New York: Oxford University Press, Incorporated, 2000. *ProQuest Ebook Central*, https://ebookcentral.proquest.com/lib/ttu/detail.action?docID=3052388. Accessed 1/25/2023.

[32] In Egypt, in the fourteenth century BCE, there was one period in which something like monotheism was practiced. The Pharaoh Amenhotep IV declared that all the temples of all the gods except Aten should be closed, and all of his subjects should worship Aten only. He then changed his name to Akhenaten ("Useful to Aten"). It is not clear whether he was claiming that Aten is the only one who is real, or that Aten is the only one who should be worshipped. After his

Israelites monotheism, but only that they should worship no god other than the god that brought them out of Egypt. Other nations have their gods, but Israel is to devote herself to only one. In the Exodus story, Moses is instructed to tell Pharaoh,

> The Lord, the God of the Hebrews, has met with us. So now, please, let us go a three days' journey into the wilderness, that we may sacrifice to the Lord our God.[33]

It is noteworthy that he calls himself "the god of the Hebrews" and "our god" rather than simply "God," While this doesn't prove that he thought gods of other peoples exist, it is an odd way to say it if Israel's God is the only one. When Saint Paul came to preach to the gentiles in Athens, he said:

> Men of Athens, I observe that you are very religious in all respects. 23For while I was passing through and examining the objects of your worship, I also found an altar with this inscription, "TO AN UNKNOWN GOD." Therefore what you worship in ignorance, this I proclaim to you.[34]

The prophet Muhammad thought a large part of his disagreement with the Meccans was on how many gods there are, and that the one God wanted them to abandon their polytheism. Either way, it seems clear that the idea that there might be more than one god was not simply incoherent. On the view that singularity is built into the meaning of the term "God," "There is more than one god," is a straightforward contradiction, entailing that there is more than one of the things there can be only one of. Most of the world at the time would have been committing an elementary error in logic. In the same vein, when Muhammad came to the people of Mecca, he explicitly claimed that their error was to believe there are many when there is in fact only one. He took himself to be disagreeing about how many things fall under the concept, not that they should wield a different concept. Every time monotheists have encountered polytheists they have taken themselves to have a real disagreement about the number of gods.

So, what have the little-g gods got in common with the big-G God of the western monotheisms? What does the word mean, such that it can apply to both Zeus and Allah?[35] Etymology gives us little help, as the words in different languages seem to point in different directions. The Indo-European languages alone have at least three roots, one pointing to ritual activities (the root of *God*

death, Egypt reverted to its previous polytheism immediately. A nice discussion of what the archeological and literary evidence shows is James K. Hoffmeier 's *Akhenaten and the Origin of Monotheism*, New York: Oxford, 2015.

[33] Exodus 3:18, New American Standard translation. The phrase "the Lord" in this verse translates the tetragrammaton, the proper name the god of the Hebrews gave to Moses.

[34] Acts 17:22–23, New American Standard translation.

[35] It's also worth noting that many other languages, if not all, have a word that functions exactly the same way. This is not especially a problem for English.

and *Gott*), one to putting things in place (the root of Slavic *Bog* and Sanskrit root *Bhaga-*), and one pointing to the bright daylight sky (the root of *Deus* and *Zeus*, among others).[36] Other language groups bring even more conceptual variety to the party.

Another possibility is to locate the essence of divinity in how it relates to the natural world. The difference between a superhuman bully and a god is primarily that the bully is part of the natural order of things. This being may come from far away, and be very different from us, but it still inhabits space-time along with us, and is subject to all the same natural laws. It may appear to be working miracles,[37] but will always be making use of the natural order, not violating it. So perhaps what makes something a god has to do with its being outside of the natural order. Sociologist Rodney Stark takes this tack when he states categorically, "Gods are supernatural beings."[38] Of course, this just pushes the problem back a step (as I argued in the last section), leaving us with the difficulty of defining "supernatural" in an informative and noncircular way. To recap, this difficulty is related to the difficulty, in philosophy of science, of defining "natural" or "physical." If we think of what is natural as what is accounted for by the physical sciences, then we are left with a choice: do we mean the natural sciences as we currently understand them? Then we must allow that future discoveries might count as supernatural because they don't fit with current science. Or do we mean the natural sciences when they are completed? Then we leave open the possibility that ghosts and gods could turn out to be natural after all (because future science might be able to account for them). Stark himself notes earlier in the same section where he tells us what he means by "god"

> All religions involve conception of the supernatural. Most people in all societies believe there is *something* that somehow is above, beyond, over, or otherwise superior to the natural world. But, beyond this vague generalization, there is unending conflict about what the supernatural is like, and intense disputes concerning what it does, if anything.[39]

A more promising direction to look would be in how people fix the reference of the term, in particular by what kind of response to them is appropriate. In all the bewildering variety of gods in the world, one commonality stands out: whatever gods are, they should be worshipped. Nelson Pike suggests that worthiness of

[36] James P. Mallory, & Adams, Douglas Q. (2006). *The Oxford Introduction to Proto-Indo-European and the Proto-Indo-European World.* Chapter 23, "Religion" New York: Oxford University Press.

[37] This is the point of Arthur Clarke's observation, "Any sufficiently advanced technology is indistinguishable from magic." *Profiles of the Future: An Inquiry into the Limits of the Possible*, New York: Harper & Row, 1973, p. 21.

[38] Rodney Stark, *One True God*, Princeton: Princeton University Press, 2001, p. 10.

[39] Stark, *One True God*, p. 9.

worship is the core of the idea: a god is something that is worthy of worship. Monotheism is the idea that there is only one of those. In other words, if there is a god, it is *the* God. "God" then, becomes a title, not a name. This suggestion ties together many threads: Pike believes that, in order to be worthy of worship, a being must be maximally excellent, and the creator of all things other than itself. But people can disagree. He expresses that thought this way:

> First, I shall assume that within the discourse of the Christian religion, the term "God" is a descriptive expression having an identifiable meaning. It is not, e.g., a proper name. As part of this first assumption, I shall suppose, further, that "God" is a very special type of descriptive expression – what I shall call a title. A title is a term used to mark a certain position or value-status as does, e.g., "Caesar" in the sentence "Hadrian is Caesar." To say that Hadrian is Caesar is to say that Hadrian occupies a certain governmental position; more specifically, it is to say that Hadrian is Emperor of Rome. To affirm of some individual that He is God is to affirm that that individual occupies some special position (e.g., that He is Ruler of the Universe) or that that individual has some special value-status (e.g., that He is a being a greater than which cannot be conceived).[40]

This idea makes the best sense of our linguistic practices as well as our religious ones and builds into the concept of god a normative requirement on human beings. Whatever a being is like, one can deny that it is a god simply by denying that it is worthy of worship. This is a frequent line of reasoning proposed by monotheists when approaching polytheists: Your many gods are defective in some way, so they are not worthy of your worship, so they are not gods after all.[41] Polytheists are making a mistake, even a logical mistake, but the mistake is failing to think hard enough about what makes something worthy of worship, not endorsing the contradiction that there are many of something there is only one of. It is certainly possible to direct your worship at unworthy objects, even knowingly, just as it is possible to desire things that are not good for you.[42]

2.2 What Does It Mean to Say There Is Only *One*?

When we list the monotheistic religions, the list always includes Judaism, Christianity, and Islam. Lists may – indeed, should – include others, but those

---

[40] Nelson Pike, "Omnipotence and God's Ability to Sin," *American Philosophical Quarterly*, 6, 3 (1969), 208–216. James Rachels makes a similar argument in "God and Human Attitudes," *Religious Studies* 7 (1971), 325–337.

[41] The Hebrew prophets frequently ridicule idols as "gods made with human hands." See Jeremiah 10:3–5 and Habakkuk 2:18–20, for example.

[42] Sharp readers will notice that we now have a problem of distinguishing what is worship, as opposed to other attitudes and expressions of submission, admiration, adoration, and so on. We could say that worship is necessarily directed at gods, but we can see the same circularity looming that we did when we were trying to define "supernatural."

three are considered paradigms. For short, they are often called the Abrahamic religions, because they all claim Abraham as the ultimate founder of the tradition they carry on. But it is also a commonplace of modern biblical scholarship that the religion of Moses was not so much monotheistic as it was monolatrous, or henotheistic. That is, we will have only one god, who will be our god, but we recognize that other tribes and nations have their own gods. This distinction is delineated nicely by Julius Wellhausen:

> It was not as if Jehovah had originally been regarded as the God of the universe, who subsequently became the God of Israel; He was primarily Israel's God, and only afterwards (very long afterwards) did He come to be regarded as the God of the universe.[43]

The distinctive thing about Israelite religion was not the claim that other gods don't exist (though such an idea begins to appear in the prophetic period), as that we must be faithful to our god and not follow after others.

Regardless of what Abraham believed (or even Moses), Judaism did end up claiming the absolute unity of God, and also his uniqueness, as illustrated by the beginning of the universal Jewish announcement, "Hear O Israel, the Lord our God, the Lord is one."[44] Today, to say that Judaism is monotheistic is to claim that, according to Judaism, there is exactly one thing worthy of worship. Christianity and Islam claim to be in the same tradition. But in addition to the paradigms, there are borderline cases.

For example, most Hindus believe that there is an all-inclusive consciousness behind physical reality, called "Brahman." This is not Brahma the god, who is a god in the ordinary sense, that is, a personal being who asks for worship and respect. Nevertheless, many Hindus are comfortable calling Brahman "God," and talk quite a bit like monotheists. Gandhi, in an essay called "Gita and Satyagraha,"[45] repeatedly refers to God in the singular, with the capital G, and never to "the gods." There is only one Brahman, after all. Should we count them among the monotheists? A lot depends on how they understand what Brahman is. In the Upanishads, where this idea is first explored, Brahman is described in two ways: first, it is the one reality behind all reality, and second, it is described as literally what we conscious beings are made of. Over and over, the teacher in the Upanishads describes the nature of

[43] Julius Wellhausen, J. S. Black, A. Menzies. *Prolegomena to the History of Ancient Israel: With a Reprint of the Article Israel from the "Encyclopaedia Britannica,"* United Kingdom: Adam & Charles Black, 1885, p. 437.

[44] From My Jewish Learning, "The Shema: How Listening Leads to Oneness," www.myjewishlearning.com/article/the-shema-how-listening-leads-to-oneness/. Accessed 1/25/2023.

[45] In Ronald Duncan. *Selected Writings of Mahatma Gandhi*, Boston: The Beacon Press, 1951, pp. 43–67.

Brahman as universal, and goes on to say to the student, "You are that." "*Tat tvam asi.*"[46] But the student is never instructed to worship Brahman, or to ask Brahman for anything, or in any way seek a relationship with Brahman; the student is only exhorted to realize that he is one with Brahman, in some deep, metaphysical way. Realization of one's union with Brahman is enlightenment and leads to release (*moksha*) from the cycle of death and rebirth, and therefore transcendence of individual identity. This is Vedanta, the ultimate truth revealed in the Vedas.

There are, of course, different schools of Vedanta, explicating the nature of Brahman in different ways. One very popular school of thought, Advaita Vedanta, posits that reality itself is non-dual. That is to say, there really is only one thing, Brahman, and so all the other things that seem to exist (like physical objects, individual people, gods, and so on) must be understood as either unreal illusions, or as somehow "really" identified with Brahman somehow. In particular, the individual personality, the living person, simply is identical with Brahman. What I really am deep down (*Atman*) simply is Brahman. But Brahman is not conceived of in personal terms. The term is grammatically neuter, whereas all the little-g gods are either male or female. The proper pronoun to use in referring to Brahman is the neuter pronoun, "it."

Likewise, in many Mahayana Buddhist sects, all of reality is understood as empty, and so "the empty" is the one reality. It is called "*Sunyata*," Sanskrit for "empty," and like Brahman, it is the ultimate object the Buddhist hopes to experience directly. It's not a person, and no person is in fact at all real. Other branches of Mahayana Buddhism speak of an all-pervading Buddha-nature in which all beings participate, the *Tathagatagarbha*. It is the fundamental reality, and is also the capacity to reach enlightenment, or achieve Buddhahood. In Chinese traditions, some speak of the Dao in the same way. It is a mysterious, elusive fabric of the universe, against which one struggles in vain, or happily cooperates with. But again, it is not a person, and there is no use praying to it, or begging it to give you an easier time of things.

In these Indian and Chinese schools of thought, it seems as though it would be a mistake to call their ideas monotheistic. Whatever is to be said about these cosmic unities, they do not seem to be things worthy of worship, or even of a type appropriate to worship. We might extend the word "God" as a kind of courtesy to apply to Brahman, or the *Tathagatagarbha*, or the Dao, as a gesture to their role as ultimate reality, but it would be a stretch to call

[46] This phrase is repeated several times in the *Chandogya Upanishad*. It is available in a great many translations and editions.

them Monotheisms. Here I would prefer to adopt Schellenberg's felicitous coinage, "ultimism."[47] Ultimism is the belief that there exists something that is ultimate metaphysically, is ultimate in inherent value, and is also of ultimate importance for our lives. Vedanta, Buddhism, and Daoism may qualify as mono-ultimisms, but not monotheisms.

Another kind of difficulty is posed by the Christian conception of God as Trinity in Unity, and Unity in Trinity. Christians steadfastly identify themselves as monotheists and condemn as heresy any idea that leans toward polytheism, but they also just as steadfastly claim that while God is one *thing*, or substance, he is also three persons. So, whereas we might exclude Hindus, Buddhists, and Daoists from the monotheist club on the grounds that their ultimates don't have any personality, it looks as though we should exclude Christians because their ultimate has too many personalities.

The problem is quite simple to explain, and there have been many ingenious attempts to solve it: If Father, Son, and Holy Spirit are each God, and are distinct from one another, there are three Gods. If Father, Son, and Holy Spirit are each God, and there is only one God, then Father, Son, and Holy Spirit are not distinct from one another. If there is only one God, and Father, Son, and Holy Spirit are distinct from one another, then at least two of them are not God. I have been mentioning Christianity as one of the world's paradigm monotheisms, but there is a prima facie problem with that classification. All the Christian creeds begin with "*Credo in unum Deum*" or its equivalent, but then almost all of them go on to qualify that claim by saying that while God is absolutely only one *substance*, He also exists in three *persons*. Christian orthodoxy through the ages has insisted that this is not a compromise with polytheism. There are not three gods, but one.[48] And yet the persons of this Trinity are distinct from one another, and each is equally God. Unfortunately, these claims seem to form an inconsistent set, so one of them must be wrong. Consider the following four claims, all of which are nonnegotiable claims of Christian theology[49]:

1) There is exactly one God.
2) The Father is God.
3) The Son is God.
4) The Father is not the Son.

---

[47] This coinage is found in John L. Schellenberg, *The Hiddenness Argument*, New York: Oxford University Press, 2015, p. 20.

[48] Though Richard Swinburne flirted with tritheism in Richard Swinburne, "Could There Be More than One God?" *Faith and Philosophy* 5, 3 (1988), 225–241.

[49] Thomas V. Morris, *The Logic of God Incarnate*, Ithaca: Cornell University Press, 1986.

If the first three claims are true, it seems to follow that the Father is the Son, which is the denial of the fourth. If the second, third, and fourth claims are true, it seems to follow that there are at least two Gods. Take any three of the claims, they seem to logically entail the denial of the fourth.[21] The easiest solution is to give up one of the claims that make up the inconsistent set, but Christian orthodoxy closes off all the easy solutions. Some Gnostics tried denying the second, claiming that the god Jesus called "Father" is not really god, but some lesser and not perfectly good being. The Arians denied the third, asserting that Jesus was not God, but rather some exalted spiritual being who, though powerful and wise, fell short of full divinity. The Sabellians denied the fourth, claiming that the persons of the trinity are not separate, but are rather ways that the one God presents himself. The doctrine of the Trinity as it is now expounded was adopted, and all those other views of the nature of God were ultimately counted as heresies.[50] Naturally, there are various sophisticated philosophical attempts to solve the problem, and many theologians are comfortable just resting in the mystery, but one thing that is not permissible is to pretend there is no problem here.

Since mainstream Christian orthodoxy requires that there is one God, the three persons are distinct from one another, and each of three persons is God, then it seems that mainstream Christian orthodoxy requires us to believe things that are inconsistent with one another. This is one of the problems that make both Jews and Muslims nervous about Christian theology. Not only are Christians flirting with polytheism with all this Trinitarian talk, but one of the persons of this Godhead is, in fact, a human being! Since Christians do insist they are monotheists, though, it is best to count the Christian idea of god as fundamentally monotheistic. Whatever happens with Christology and Trinitarian theology (and some of the things that happen there have a peculiarly polytheistic flavor), I think we should take the church's centuries long sincere expression of monotheism in all her creeds at face value and call them monotheists.

2.3 Summary

So, to qualify as a monotheism, a religion must require belief in exactly one being who is worthy of worship. It is to be distinguished from atheism and polytheism, even when the polytheist raises one god above all others. It is also to be distinguished from monism, the belief that all of reality is comprehended by

[50] A good popular discussion of the development of the doctrine, including the various heretical interpretations, can be found in Bart Ehrman's *How Jesus Became God: The Exaltation of a Jewish Preacher from Galilee*, New York: Harper One, 2014.

one being, when that One is not a person, and so can't be worthy of our worship. Monotheism is the idea that there is exactly one personal being worthy of worship. I will leave unanalyzed what sorts of behavior count as worship, but will presume, with most monotheists in history, that a being worthy of receiving it must be morally good, wise, and powerful. Many monotheist thinkers raise those qualities to their ultimate extent, and that is a reasonable theological move to make, but it is not part of the concept of God. Whether a being that is three persons in one substance qualifies as one God is a problem I leave for partisans to debate.

3 The Value of Experiences of God

People have clearly had and reported experiences of the one God.[51] A reasonable question to ask at this point might be, "So what?" Those people (for the most part) believe their experience is veridical. Some other people believe their reports. Others believe the whole thing is a mass of delusions, illusions, and outright hallucinations. Is there any way to adjudicate between those who accept the experiences as real and the those who reject them? We could think of the question as one of whether at least some of the people claiming to have encountered God have good reason to think so or not. Is it reasonable for them to accept the experiences, or are they being irrational in some way? This has been a lively topic of concern to philosophers at least since William James's *Varieties of Religious Experience*.[52] He concluded that they do, in fact, provide evidence for what he calls the "religious hypothesis," but only for the subjects of the experiences; they hold "no authority" for others. In recent years, some philosophers have argued that religious experience is a kind of evidence like other experiential evidence and should be treated the same way. The question remains with no consensus as to an answer. One aspect of religious experience that is frequently overlooked[53] is the fact that these experiences take place in the setting of a religion, which is, in the ordinary case, a social institution. The subjects of the experiences take part in ceremonies and rituals with other people who share, at least in part, their beliefs and convictions. This social setting contributes an important background for understanding what religious experiences are, and so what epistemic value they have.

[51] The bulk of this chapter is taken, with small changes, from "Meaning and Value in Religious Experience," in Paul Moser and Chad Meister (eds.), the *Cambridge Companion to Religious Experience*, New York: Cambridge University Press, 2020.

[52] William James, *The Varieties of Religious Experience*, New York: New American Library, 1902/1958.

[53] William Alston's *Perceiving God: The Epistemology of Religious Experience* is a notable exception to this neglect.

3.1 Religious Experience in Its Social Setting

Since a religion is a kind of social institution or practice, to understand religious experiences requires understanding them in their settings. Even though the experience itself purports to be a one-on-one encounter between the subject and the religious reality, the experience only makes sense in the context of the institution that the subject calls home. Religious experiences are not, by and large, self-interpreting. This is often taken as a special feature of religious experiences that shows why they are epistemically inferior to other experiential grounds of belief, but this is a misunderstanding of how perception works.

Suppose we want to ask what makes an experience suitable grounds for a belief. Historically, when philosophers have asked this about sensory experience, they give a list of reasons why sense-experience can be trusted, including that we can predict future experiences based on past ones; our sense experiences tell a coherent story, in a way that dreams, for example, don't; our individual senses confirm one another; and we can check our own experiences against other people's. The best explanation for these features of our experiences is that they are delivering accurate information about the world.[54] Even when they do fool us, by illusion, hallucination, or the like, one or more of those features will be absent; we can check and correct our beliefs using our other sensory beliefs and the beliefs of others. Religious experiences can't do the same. So, it seems that while sensory experience responds to checks and confirmation, religious experience doesn't, so while sensory experience is a legitimate source of belief, religious experience isn't.[55]

This picture oversimplifies what happens both in sensory experience and religious experience. To illustrate, consider this example of a typical religious experience.

> Anna has committed some small wrong (say, petty theft) and feels bad about it. She consults her mother, who says. "You know God doesn't want you to do that. It's a sin. Your conscience is telling you that." Anna decides to pray to God and ask for forgiveness. While she is praying, she feels that God is forgiving her and comforting her, while at the same time giving her courage to confess to the person she wronged and make amends. When asked about her prayer experience, she says, "I felt God's presence, both convicting me of sin and forgiving me." The members of her church confirm and accept her report as true and genuine, because that is what they would expect to happen, given their tradition's interpretation of the scripture, how it comports with their own experiences, and by the effect it has had on Anna's behavior.

[54] John Locke famously gives this argument for the general reliability of sense experience in his *Essay Concerning Human Understanding,* Book IV, chapter 11.

[55] See Richard M. Gale, "Swinburne's Argument from Religious Experience," in Alan G. Padgett (ed.), *Reason and the Christian Religion*, New York: Clarendon Press, 1994. pp. 39–63; and Nick Zangwill, "The Myth of Religious Experience," *Religious Studies* 40, 1 (2004), 1–22.

Resources provided by Anna's religious community have entered into the evaluation of the experience in several ways. First, the experience comes to her because of something she does, prompted by guidance from her community. They believe, for lots of reasons, the way to deal with sin is to confess it to God and ask for forgiveness, and that forgiveness will come. Also, when she describes the experience, she uses both ordinary language and the specialized conceptual apparatus of her religion. She describes what she was doing as prayer to God, not just talking in solitude. She describes the feeling as being comforted, not just feeling better. And finally, when she reports her experience, her coreligionists compare it to what they would expect, given their complex picture of God and His relations to the world, a picture developed over centuries. The social setting of Anna's experience provides checks and tests, all of which her experience passes. Compare Anna with another case, Bill.

> Bill is walking down the street in New York City and sees a man who looks like Ben Vereen. Being a big fan of musical theater, he recognizes him, and approaches him. The man confirms that he is indeed Ben Vereen, and after a brief chat about plays and movies, Ben autographs Bill's tourist map, and they part ways. When he gets back to Lubbock, Bill tells his theater friends about his encounter. They accept his story, saying, "Yes, Ben Vereen is known to be very friendly with fans, and he is in New York right now for the new production of *Cats*."

In other words, Bill's experience comes to him because of actions he has taken, that put him in a position to have experiences he might not otherwise have (going to New York and walking outside), and his sensory report is informed by knowledge he already has (what Ben Vereen looks like, plus his memories of Mr. Vereen's various parts in plays and movies), checked by background facts that are known to his community (yes, Mr. Vereen was in New York at the time, and the person's behavior comports with what is known about Mr. Vereen's character), and supported by what they would expect to happen, based on what they know about New York and Ben Vereen.

In other words, religious experiences are subject to the same kinds of check for coherence with a broader theory as sensory experiences are. Even fairly typical, everyday sensory beliefs are subject to background beliefs and community checks. When I form a simple belief based on my visual experience first thing in the morning, a huge amount of socially provided support goes into the formation of the belief. I identify my surroundings as my own home (this is not a given, since I do sometimes travel and wake up disoriented in strange places). I don't ask myself if this is home, I simply form the belief that it is, informed more or less automatically by my other beliefs about what I would expect to see in my room. I don't reason to that conclusion; the background information contributes to the content of the belief I form. Since it is unremarkable, I don't report it to anyone, so checks are not needed. There are significant differences between how religious experiences ground beliefs and how sensory experiences ground beliefs, but the differences are not as great as they seem at first glance.

3.2 Doxastic Practice Epistemology

Even though lots of aspects of religious experience seem to match up with similar facts about sense-perception, there is still reason to be dubious about it, and so to treat it differently. For one thing, sensory experiences tend to be informationally rich, and provide us with new information almost constantly, whereas religious experiences tend to be informationally scant compared to sensory experiences, and rarely cause their subjects to change their beliefs about the nature of the purported reality they experience. This means that prior theoretical knowledge and background belief have a much larger role to play in religious experiences. Also, there seems to be one common view of the physical world (different in details from person to person, to be sure, but almost unanimous in broad outline), while religious experiences figure in wildly different and mutually inconsistent stories about their objects.

Because there are significant differences between the two kinds of experiences, there may be significant differences between the kinds of beliefs they can ground. We do take our sensory experiences to be good grounds for beliefs about the world, even while we recognize them to be fallible and corrigible. Should we take religious experiences to be good grounds for belief, too, in spite of the differences from sense-experience, or should we reject them as unfit for grounding belief, in spite of the similarities? The question comes down to asking if the experiences are reliable indications of some reality.

The most obvious way to undercut the credibility of an experiential claim is to have evidence that the object of the experience doesn't exist, or more generally, that the belief formed is simply false. Returning to the example of Bill, above, if I happened to know that Ben Vereen was not in New York at that time, then I have reason to believe Bill's belief is false, and so there was something wrong with the experience that misled him. It may be no fault of Bill's. Perhaps there is a Ben Vereen double wandering around the city fooling Vereen fans. To undercut a belief formed on the basis of religious experience in the same way, I would have to have evidence that a corresponding religious doctrine is false.[56] So if a person reports an experience in which she feels God forgiving her, we would have to have reason to believe that God is, in fact, not

[56] This is part of what Plantinga means by a *de facto* objection to religious belief. See *Warranted Christian Belief*, p. ix.

forgiving her. Staunch defenders of the atheistic argument from evil might say that we do have conclusive reason to believe that God does not exist, so all beliefs about divine beliefs, desires, or dispositions must be false. Apart from something like that, though, there is no general refuting defeater for religious belief.

A second way is to find reason to believe that there is something wrong with the way the belief was formed. Perhaps the mechanisms are defective, and so unreliable. If we know from the past that Bill can't distinguish faces very well, then we will have doubts about any of his reports about whom he has seen. So how do we go about discovering whether the religious-experience way of forming beliefs is defective? We can't just say that it is not like sensory experience. While it is true (as we noted above) that there are significant differences, we also noted that the differences are not as great as they seem on first glance. Even if the differences were huge, we need further argument to show that those differences are disabling for religious experience. In other words, we need reason to think that the characteristics of sense-experience with which we are so impressed are necessary for other kinds of experience in order for them to be good grounds for belief.

Showing that a source of beliefs is reliable is a tricky task, because to do that is to show that the beliefs so formed are true, by and large. Religious experience seems to be in trouble here, because it is, ultimately, the only source for beliefs about God, or emptiness, or Atman, or whatever. We can't let the practice of forming beliefs from religious experience be a witness in its own case, since its reliability is precisely what is in question. In general, if a source of beliefs is the only source for beliefs of that type, then there is no way for the source to prove itself reliable, on pain of circularity. If the source is not the only one for a particular kind of content, then it can be supported by the other sources for that content. For example, if vision tells us there is a fire in front of us, it can be confirmed by the sound of burning, the smell of smoke, the feeling of heat, and so on. But it's not all clear for sense-perception. True, the senses all support each other, by and large, but what supports the bunch of them? Sense-perception generally seems to be in the same bind; it can't show itself to be reliable without presuming itself to be reliable.[57]

But that's not the end of the matter. We may not be able to show a source of beliefs reliable, in a noncircular way, but we can certainly show one to be unreliable. If a source produces two contradictory beliefs, we know one of them is false, even if we don't know which one. If a source of beliefs produces lots of contradictions, then its ratio of true beliefs to false beliefs approaches 50/50, and

[57] William Alston makes this case in *Perceiving God: The Epistemology of Religious Experience.*

it's fair to call it unreliable. Wishful thinking, astrology, taking auspices, and such don't have an impressive track record, so the epistemically careful have abandoned them as not reliable. If we show a source of beliefs is unreliable, it's no longer a good idea to rely on it. If we fail to show it to be unreliable, then it has passed a sort of minimal test, and so it may be rational to rely on it after all. Failing to run into contradictions suggests that the source is on to some mind-independent reality. Does religious experience fall into that category? Does it escape producing massive contradictions?

Looking at religious experiences within particular traditions, they seem to be more or less consistent. Theravada monks tend to come out of their meditative states with very similar beliefs about the nature of reality as impermanent and unsatisfactory. Christian mystics come away from contemplative prayer with roughly the same story about God's love and majesty. There are anomalies, but that's to be expected from any source of beliefs. But the same question that arises for the senses generally arises for religious experience generally: while the individual religions escape massive contradictions, they do not escape massively contradicting one another. On the Alstonian reasoning I have been deploying, this shows that religious experience *tout court* is not a reliable way of forming beliefs. But perhaps the individual religious traditions can claim that theirs, at least, escapes contradictions internally, and so it's rational to rely on them. Even if they all escape contradiction individually, they still contradict one another, so they can't all be reliable, but if each is internally consistent, then it can be rational to engage in one of them.

We noted earlier that our five senses prop each other up, evidentially. Suppose that was not true. Suppose, for example, that vision produced a consistent, clear picture of the world, but it didn't match up with the other senses at all. So, we see a fire, but we feel cold, hear a buzzing, and smell roses. And just to up the ante, let's suppose that the unreliable senses give us something different every time. So the next time we see a fire, we might feel prickles, hear hissing, and smell skunk. We would quickly come to see that our senses are not, as a whole, reliable. On the other hand, we would come to see that vision is at least constant and consistent and learn to ignore the others. We might do the same if one tradition's religious experiences were constant and consistent, and all the others were unreliable.

Now imagine if each of the senses gave us a constant, consistent picture of the world, but the individual senses didn't give us the *same* consistent picture. Each sense would have some claim to being a legitimate source of belief, but we would have no idea which, if any, was the right one. Is vision showing us the truth, while the other senses are unreliable, or is hearing the truth-revealing sense, while the others are deceptive? This is like our situation with respect to religious experience; we have no independent way to show it is reliably representing reality. The analogy with sense-experience is far from perfect; nevertheless, they do seem to be analogous in the epistemically important ways: neither religious experience nor sensory experience can be demonstrated (in a noncircular way) to be reliable; both sense-perception generally and at least some individual religious traditions' experiential claims escape massive self-contradiction, and so are not revealed by their own deliverances to be unreliable. So, if it can be reasonable to rely on our senses to form beliefs, it can also be reasonable to form religious beliefs on the basis of religious experiences.

3.3 The Common Core Hypothesis

In spite of the apparent contradictions among religious-experience reports, and the resulting differences in the religious doctrines formed from them, some still believe that all religious experiences are of a single reality, and that the differences are superficial, or otherwise explainable. Since there is so much overlap among the religions on moral values, some think that the metaphysics of the being behind them all is much less important, so it is possible that all the religions are in contact, via religious experience, with the same fundamental reality. One such theory is espoused by John Hick.[58]

The view starts from the idea that religious experiences across the different traditions are equally well grounded, epistemically, and so the believers in them are equally rational. On the other hand, believers in each tradition are aware of this fact, and so are aware that people in other traditions are equally rational. In particular, they are aware that they have no special reason to prefer their own experiential evidence over that of others. But they also have no reason to abandon their own experiences. The only remaining possibility is that all the subjects of religious experiences are in contact with the same reality (Hick calls it "the Real"), and that reality is ambiguous. In particular, it can be experienced as personal, as the theistic religions aver, or as impersonal, as many Chinese and Indian religions assert. Thus, these different experiences can be of the same Real, and those who have the experiences (and those who believe them) can be equally rational. Clearly, the variety of claims about the Real cannot all be true, but the experiences in all their variety are, in some sense, all veridical. Hick's view is that the Real as it is in itself is beyond all our categories, incapable of being adequately described in human language, and that is why it can be conceptualized in such different ways.

---

[58] John Hick, *An Interpretation of Religion*.

Hick's view has not attracted a lot of support, largely because it is hard to say what the Real is, as it is in itself, if none of our concepts apply to it.[59] But one need not be a pluralist like Hick to believe that there is a common core to religious experiences. Even apart from the idea that religious experiences are all of the same reality, there is an idea that they all support a common (admittedly thin) component of religious belief. Take what William James refers to as the "Religious Hypothesis":

> [R]eligion says essentially two things. First, she says that the best things are the more eternal things, the overlapping things, the things in the universe that throw the last stone, so to speak, and say the final word. ... The second affirmation of religion is that we are better off, even now, if we believe her first affirmation to be true.[60]

This hypothesis is meager at best, as it gives us no guidance about what those eternal things are, or why they are the best things. This is the general problem with Common Core views. They save the evidential value of religious experiences as to the thin common core but leave us with nothing to say about the more detailed contents of the experiences. No religious disagreements can be settled this way. No discovery can be made about God, or Brahman, or the Dao, that is not undermined by an equal and opposite experience elsewhere. The best views like this can do is reassure us that those details don't matter. Such a verdict would be a major revision in any religion's self-understanding.

3.4 Background Information

One reason that different religious traditions end up with utterly different interpretations of religious experiences is that the background beliefs they bring to the experience are very different. We noted earlier that even my ordinary perceptual beliefs depend on background information, which contribute to identifying the objects in my environment and making predictions about what I will experience in the near future. It's because I have beliefs, formed long ago and lying latent in my cognitive structures, about the nature of glass and tile floors that I confidently expect to hear a crash when I drop a glass in my kitchen. In addition to general knowledge about objects and materials, I also have individual knowledge of my own past that contributes to my identifying this house as mine, and that woman as my wife. Vast theoretical structures about the world and my own place in it are already in place in my mind when I have a new

[59] Daniel Howard-Snyder explains the problem in detail in his "Who or What Is God, According to John Hick?" *Topoi* 36 (2017), 571–586.

[60] William James, "The Will to Believe," in Alburey Castell (ed.), *Essays in Pragmatism*, New York: Hafner Press, 1948, p. 105.

perceptual experience, and it's because of those structures that I am able to form new beliefs so automatically and incorporate them so effortlessly into my body of knowledge. Much of that structure is provided to me by the social group I grew up in. Some of what I know is based on my own experience, but by far the biggest portion is provided by others. Everything I know about the past, except for the most meager facts about my own biography, I learned in school and from books. The same is true of geography, astronomy, physics, biology, chemistry, and practically anything else worth knowing. A person who set out to build a body of knowledge based only on what he or she can come to know on his or her own cognitive resources would not be able to get very far.[61]

The same is true, to an even greater extent, about religious experience, and this accounts for a lot of the variety in reports of religious experience. Religious experiences come to people in religious traditions, by and large, and each is quite naturally described in the language of its tradition. Given that religious experiences are frequently vague and not generally rich in detail, it is natural that they would be filled in with background beliefs about the object in question, just as the famous Hidden Dalmatian picture[62] can appear very different after the addition of background information. While this fact seems to undercut the evidential value of the experiences, in that it implies that a lot of reported content doesn't come from the experience itself, it also weakens the objection based on the variety of reports, by providing a non–ad hoc explanation for the variety. This informational poverty is exactly what one should expect of encounters with the transcendent. The content of the experience itself is so sparse that background beliefs must provide a larger portion of the resultant belief's content. So, reliance on the testimony of others, and the theoretical models built up over generations, is integral to the understanding of religious experiences.

3.5 Meaning

Even if we grant that it is possible for religious experiences to be good grounds for belief, it is still an open question whether they have any value to human lives. The role of background belief and social setting provide a clue to an answer. Perhaps the most important area in which social context provides an important component for religious experience is in the realm of meaning, both

[61] This fact is described thoroughly in Cecil A. J. Coady, *Testimony: A Philosophical Study*.

[62] The Hidden Dalmatian illusion consists of an array of black spots on a white background, which does not appear to make a picture. When a viewer is told that there is a dog in the picture, they suddenly resolve some of the dots into a shape of a dog. Once you have seen the dog, you can't return to seeing the picture as just an array of dots. It is explained nicely in Richard Gregory's *Intelligent Eye*, New York: McGraw Hill, 1971.

in the sense of linguistic (or other semantic) meaning, and in the sense of significance. Obviously, linguistic meaning is a social matter, as it is a conventional matter. The same goes for religious language. The meanings of all the key terms used in describing religious experiences are words whose meanings are fixed in the same kind of conventional way as the terms of ordinary language. Many religious terms, in fact, come from ordinary language, and are applied by analogy in religious contexts. How exactly that works is a much-debated question, and one outside the scope of this work. According to the most popular theories of mental content, the same can be said for the semantics, if any, of mental items. Meaning and reference are fixed partly with the help of others, outside your own head.[63]

There is still a concern about how purely religious language and can get their meaning, since there seems to be no independent access to the objects so that users of the language can come to agreement about the extension of terms.[64] The same concern arises even for the religious components of analogical language and thought. If there is no public standard for what the terms refer to, then how can we establish any common usage? Analogy does give us a partial inroad but doesn't answer the worry totally. We might, from a religious experience, form the belief that we had just encountered a very wise, very powerful, holy being, who is also very loving and concerned about us. While the terms "wise," "powerful," and "loving" don't apply to God literally, we can see how they might be extended by analogy. But what about "holy"? We can define the term, but it's hard to see how it connects with any properties that can be represented in the phenomenology of an experience. It is difficult to see how any experience could have the right kind of content to ground religious language. There are a whole host of terms that fit together in the same way. Perhaps they can be interdefined, so that religious language forms a coherent conceptual system, but it's not at all obvious how they can be grounded in experience.

It turns out we have other realms of meaning with the same isolated character; their concepts can be interdefined, but they can't be defined in terms whose meaning comes from outside that closed circle. Color language – by which I mean the ordinary language of colors we experience, not reflectances or wavelengths – are perfectly meaningful, but there is no way to explain what

[63] This fact shows us the way to answer Islamophobic concerns about whether Muslims worship the same God as Christians and Jews. If reference is fixed the way most of us think it is, then it is enough that Jesus was intentionally talking about the God of Moses, and so was Muhammad. Differences in theology don't, in general, make for differences in reference.

[64] This concern is parallel to the no-public-checks worry about the epistemic status of beliefs based on religious experience.

red is without using color language.[65] But we still use the language unproblematically, because we have fairly good agreement about the extensions of the terms. In other words, because the vast majority of us see colors the same way, we can agree on how to use the terms, and we can teach them to others. Likewise, moral language is not definable in nonmoral language (though naturalists keep trying). But as in the case of color language, there is vast agreement on what is good and bad, right and wrong, virtuous and vicious. This sounds surprising, because our moral talk tends to come into play in the cases in which we disagree, but there is a background of agreement that is vastly bigger than the areas of contention.[66] It's as if we never spoke about color at all except in borderline cases when it is vague or unclear, or when we are talking to colorblind people. Again, the background of agreement makes it possible for us to apply terminology and teach it to new learners. It seems that we cannot say the same for religious language, precisely because there is no widespread agreement about the objects of experience. There is agreement within particular traditions, and even among closely related traditions, but no universal religious experience, beyond the two general components of James's "religious hypothesis." There seems to be no clear way to give universally accessible content to religious talk.

James's way of talking about the core of religious experiences does, however, give a way to talk about another aspect of meaning, what we might call "significance." Part of what a community provides for those who have religious experiences is a sense of the importance of those experiences, and related matters, for living their lives. One way it does this is by providing additional reasons to try to be a good person and do good in the world. While it may be problematic to try to make moral value dependent on religious truths,[67] it is certainly the case that religions regularly make recommendations about how to be good. They also provide a story about a cosmic order in which goodness matters; it is no longer just a matter of the individual endorsing values and trying to live by them. The religious community reinforces that connection with moral

---

65 This is why inverted spectra and the story of Mary, the blind color scientist provides such interesting puzzles. See Alex Byrne, "Inverted Qualia," *The Stanford Encyclopedia of Philosophy* (Winter Ed.), Edward N. Zalta (ed.), 2018, https://plato.stanford.edu/archives/win2018/entries/qualia-inverted/. For Mary and the Knowledge Argument, see Jackson, Frank, "Epiphenomenal Qualia," *Philosophical Quarterly* 32 (1982), 127–136, and the huge literature that followed.

66 In the appendix to *The Abolition of Man*, London: Oxford University Press, 1943, C. S. Lewis lists a large number of citations from different cultures to illustrate the vast background agreement on values.

67 See Geoff Sayre-McCord, "Metaethics," *The Stanford Encyclopedia of Philosophy* (Summer Ed.), Edward N. Zalta (ed.), 2014, https://plato.stanford.edu/archives/sum2014/entries/metaethics/, especially section two, "The Euthyphro Problem."

value, and so helps the individual live up the values he or she sees as reaching beyond the self. It is no accident that so many religious experiences, especially conversion experiences, come with a recognition of one's previous life as morally inadequate, and a resolution to do better.

In a similar way, religious experiences can provide a sense of meaning or significance to one's life. In contrast to a naturalistic view, according to which a human life is not the sort of thing that can have meaning (or if it does, it is chosen by the individual), religions generally offer a story about what matters about human life, and roots that value in something outside of and greater than the individual.[68] According to the Catholic Catechism, God "calls man to seek him, to know him, to love him with all his strength."[69] This goal underwrites the whole orientation of a Catholic life, in understanding and obeying the will of God. According to Theravada Buddhists, the goal of all life is to bring an end to suffering by seeking enlightenment, and a human life is a precious opportunity to pursue it.[70] This goal underwrites the Theravada Buddhist story about what is good and bad, and the social organizations of monks and laypeople, and their complex relations to one another. In both cases, these claims about the nature of human existence play a fundamental role in their respective views on how we should live. Just as the individual's efforts to do good and be good take on greater richness as part of the cosmic story, so does the individual's life take on greater meaning as part of a cosmic story in which it has a purpose. The religious community provides the individual with the bulk of that story to function as theoretical framework and background information for interpreting experiences, and also provides behavioral support for efforts to orient one's life appropriately, according to that story.

3.6 Conclusion

Religious experiences are often conceived of as something that happens to the individual, and are private, inaccessible to examination by others. Nothing could be further from the truth. On examination, we can see that religious experiences happen to individuals in social groups, and the social setting is essential to a great many aspects of the importance of those experiences. Yes, the "experience" part – the qualia or what have you – is thought to be private,

---

[68] I argued for something like this in "Religious Experience as Doubt Resolution," *International Journal for Philosophy of Religion* 18 (1985), 81–86.

[69] *Catechism of the Catholic Church.* Vatican City: Libreria Editrice Vaticana, 1993. www.vatican.va/archive/ENG0015/__P1.HTM. Accessed 7/28/2023.

[70] Thanissaro Bikkhu, "Chiggala Sutta: The Hole" (SN 56.48), translated from the Pali by Thanissaro Bhikkhu. *Access to Insight (BCBS Ed.)*, July 1, 2010, www.accesstoinsight.org/tipitaka/sn/sn56/sn56.048.than.html. Accessed 7/28/2023.

just in the way that sense-data are private, but there is a lot more than mere qualitative experience happening. Just as sensory experiences start with qualia and are heavily processed with information from other sources before they eventuate in beliefs, and much of that processing is public and social, so religious experiences are socially embedded. That social embedding provides background information, used to interpret the experience; confirmation from other members of the community, which enriches the experience's evidential value; and meaning, which gives richness to religious belief and purpose to human life.

4 Where Religious Experience Fits in the Grounds of Religious Belief

Granting that religious experiences of the one God can happen and can provide evidential grounding for religious beliefs, it still remains to be explained how that information contributes to the grounding of the large and complex doctrinal systems of Christianity, Judaism, and Islam. Our picture of the world is constantly updated by sensory experience, but religious belief systems seem to remain relatively static. Even if people are constantly having religious experiences, those experiences seem to contribute relatively little to the doctrinal systems themselves. Even if we grant that there is nothing unreasonable about the idea of an experiential encounter with God as conceived by Christianity, or even that the experiences can give evidence for their resultant beliefs, there is still a concern about whether such experiences can contribute anything *distinctive* to Christian doctrine. The same goes for all the Abrahamic religions.

Christianity was, early on, based on the religious experiences of the disciples. The gospels cite visions of the risen Christ as proof of his resurrection, and so as confirmation of his teachings:

> And they left the tomb quickly with fear and great joy and ran to report it to His disciples. And behold, Jesus met them and greeted them. And they came up and took hold of His feet and worshiped Him. Then Jesus *said to them, "Do not be afraid; go and take word to My brethren to leave for Galilee, and there they will see Me."[71]
>
> nd behold, two of them were going that very day to a village named Emmaus, which was about seven miles from Jerusalem. And they were talking with each other about all these things which had taken place. While they were talking and discussing, Jesus Himself approached and began traveling with them. But their eyes were prevented from recognizing Him.[72]

[71] Matthew 28:8–10, New American Standard translation.
[72] Luke 24:13–16, New American Standard translation.

Originally, Mark's gospel did not contain an account of the risen Christ. The account that appears in our modern Bibles was a later addition. The apostle Paul became a Christian after a particularly compelling religious experience:

> Now Saul, still breathing threats and murder against the disciples of the Lord, went to the high priest, and asked for letters from him to the synagogues at Damascus, so that if he found any belonging to the Way, both men and women, he might bring them bound to Jerusalem. As he was traveling, it happened that he was approaching Damascus, and suddenly a light from heaven flashed around him; 4and he fell to the ground and heard a voice saying to him, "Saul, Saul, why are you persecuting Me?" And he said, "Who are You, Lord?" And He said, "I am Jesus whom you are persecuting."[73]

And in his own words:

> For you have heard of my former manner of life in Judaism, how I used to persecute the church of God beyond measure and tried to destroy it; and I was advancing in Judaism beyond many of my contemporaries among my countrymen, being more extremely zealous for my ancestral traditions. But when God, who had set me apart even from my mother's womb and called me through His grace, was pleased to reveal His Son in me so that I might preach Him among the Gentiles, I did not immediately consult with flesh and blood, nor did I go up to Jerusalem to those who were apostles before me; but I went away to Arabia, and returned once more to Damascus.[74]

As we can see from Paul's account, a religious experience can include a direct revelation, so we mustn't fall into the trap of thinking that religious experiences can't be contentful, even if they are nowhere near as informationally rich as sensory experiences.[75] We can grant the disciples and Paul were sincere and truthful, and so their experiences were good grounds for their individual beliefs, many of which became orthodox Christian doctrine.

Christianity has a very rich idea of what God is like. But when theologians justify religious doctrines, they almost always appeal to scripture and reasoning, never to individual experiences. As we saw in Section 2, background beliefs provide a lot of the justification for beliefs based on religious experience. They give a framework for interpreting experiences and confirmation of some of those background beliefs. It seems that religious doctrines come ultimately from the religious experiences of someone, but the transmission of those beliefs depends entirely on testimony. That is, the ones who didn't see the risen Christ have to trust the ones who did. Given this account, two things follow: 1)

[73] Acts 9:1–5, New American Standard translation.

[74] Galatians 1:13–17, New American Standard translation.

[75] In Galatians 1:11–12, Paul denies that he got the gospel he preaches from any human, but instead that it was revealed to him by Jesus Christ.

Religious experience provides part of the ground of religious belief in the beginning of a religion; and 2) Religious experience does not provide *all* of the grounds of particular beliefs. What, then, does religious experience contribute?

Before we can answer that question, it would be helpful to make some distinctions and respond to a few prima facie problems with this account. First, there is a difference between the ground of a religious doctrine, as believed by many over time, and the grounds of an individual's belief in that doctrine. Presumably, the grounds for a religious doctrine will include some reports of religious experience, but a great deal of it is based on inference from testimony. To oversimplify for the sake of clarity, it goes something like this: theologians take statements in scripture, which are taken to be nonnegotiable, and reason from them. They derive what they take to be logical consequences from those statements. For example, take the Roman Catholic doctrine of purgatory. There is no direct reference or description of such a place anywhere in the Bible. Instead, it was inferred from a story in the apocryphal book of 2 Maccabees.[76] In this story, Judas Maccabaeus has come out to a battlefield to retrieve the bodies of the dead. When he sees that some of them were wearing forbidden amulets, he urges his soldiers to pray for the forgiveness of their sins. It is reasoned that the only way this makes sense is if their souls are in a place where their eternal fate is not yet settled, and there is hope for their salvation.

Believers also sometimes derive new doctrines when putting two or more different pieces of scripture together, to derive a new doctrine not itself contained any of those scriptures. The Devil, the great adversary of God, is identified by Christians as identical to the serpent in the Garden of Eden, who tempted Eve; Satan, the adversary in the book of Job; and the "Lucifer, son of the morning" in Isaiah 14:12. There is no reason to take these three to be same, or to think that the Satan of Job is evil; these identifications were made later.[77] It is not uncommon that early Christian thinkers identify different characters in the Bible as one and the same, just as the woman taken in adultery in the Gospel of John came to be identified with Mary Magdalene, though the text does not support such an identification.

Just as doctrine may begin with accounts of experiences but is elaborated by various kinds of reasoning and interpretation, so it goes with an individual believer. An individual's personal religious beliefs will depend almost entirely

[76] 2 Maccabees 12:42–45.

[77] For a nice discussion of the development of the idea of Satan, see Elaine Pagels's *Adam, Eve and the Serpent: Sex and Politics in Early Christianity*, New York: Vintage Books, 1989; and *The Origin of Satan: How Christians Demonized Jews, Pagans, and Heretics*, New York: Vintage Books, 1995.

on testimony from scripture and other believers. A person born today, if she acquires any religious beliefs at all, will almost certainly acquire the beliefs of her parents and larger community. Those beliefs are then nurtured by whatever religious institutions she is associated with and is taught by them. Testimony then looms very large in the justification of religious beliefs. Guy Axtell argues all religious beliefs today come from choosing an authority and accepting their testimony, and there is no external justification for choosing one authority over another. If Axtell is right, then if an individual's beliefs are true, it a matter of what Axtell calls "religious luck." Typically, a person believes what her community believes, and so it is a matter of geographical accident that the ones who are right are right, and the ones who are wrong are wrong.[78]

But, *pace* Axtell, we granted above that religious experiences can provide confirmation of doctrines. Many Christians find that their experiences of God confirm their conviction that God is loving. For example, see the case of Mr. Finney, in James's Varieties of Religious Experience. He describes his experience of the Holy Spirit descending upon him as being like "waves and waves of liquid love."[79] Others describe experiences of being convicted of sin, confirming their belief that God is just and holy. So religious experience still forms part of the grounds of that person's beliefs. But what the person believes comes largely from the background beliefs provided by the doctrines of the community, so it seems that doctrines are partly grounded in religious experiences, but those experiences are partly grounded in doctrine. That seems like circular reasoning, and in a way it is. It is an example of what William Alston calls "epistemic circularity."[80] That is to say, the grounding isn't logically circular, but the grounding of the belief depends on the presupposition that the grounding background beliefs are well-grounded. Whatever story we tell about the development of doctrine, it applies to the background beliefs themselves. So, when a person forms beliefs about God based on religious experiences, that belief depends in large part in the very belief about God that is being confirmed.

Alston argues that such epistemic circularity need not undermine a piece of reasoning, and that in fact, an epistemically circular bit of reasoning can justify a belief, so the grounding of religious beliefs partly on background beliefs need not be undermined by it. But he also counsels caution when he says:

[78] Guy Axtell, *Problems of Religious Luck: Assessing the Limits of Reasonable Religious Disagreement*, Lanham, : Lexington Books/Rowman & Littlefield, 2019.

[79] William James, *The Varieties of Religious Experience: A Study in Human Nature Being the Gifford Lectures on Natural Religion Delivered at Edinburgh in 1901–1902*, pp. 254–256.

[80] William P. Alston, "Epistemic Circularity," *Philosophy and Phenomenological Research* 47, (1986); Reprinted in *Epistemic Justification: Essays in the Theory of Knowledge*. Ithaca: Cornell University Press, 1989: 319–349. The idea takes a prominent role in his defense of religious experience in *Perceiving God.*

> Epistemic circularity does not in and of itself disqualify the argument. But even granting this point, the argument will not do its job unless we *are* justified in accepting its premises; and that is the case only if sense perception is in fact reliable. This is to offer a stone instead of bread. We can say the same of any belief-forming practice whatever, no matter how disreputable. We can just as well say of crystal ball gazing that if it *is* reliable, we can use a track-record argument to show that it is reliable. But when we ask whether one or another source of belief is reliable, we are interested in *discriminating* those that can be reasonably trusted from those that cannot. Hence merely showing that *if* a given source is reliable it can be shown by its record to be reliable, does nothing to indicate that the source belongs to the sheep rather that with the goats.[81]

In other words, epistemic circularity seems problematic in the same way logical circularity is, and so an epistemically circular argument gives no evidential support for its conclusion. But as long as the premises of the argument are justified, and the argument is valid, then the argument does in fact confer justification on the conclusion. This seems odd, because it seems to mean that epistemically circular reasoning can show only that if a belief is well grounded, then it is well grounded. All we can retrieve is some reason to think our beliefs are coherent. Nevertheless, if we disqualify epistemically circular reasoning, we are left with nothing to say about whether our beliefs are justified or not. But showing how beliefs are logically articulated is not nothing, and when talking about entire belief-forming systems, demonstrations of logical articulation are the best we can get. Alston's view is that, at an appropriate level of generality, the only evidence we can supply for our belief-forming practices come from the practices themselves, so arguments based on religious experience are ineluctably epistemically circular, but at least religious experience is no worse off epistemically than any other way of forming beliefs.

To give a case study of how this sort of thing transpires, two doctrines that are distinctive of Christianity, the Incarnation and the Trinity, can serve as illustrations of the process of doctrinal development. By the end of the first century, the majority of Christians agreed that Jesus was God in the flesh.[82] There were still dissenters who called themselves Christians, and even among those who agreed, there were still finicky details to be worked out. There was also agreement that God is somehow three persons in one substance, though the same caveats apply. Before that, for most of the first century, there were a variety of views on the nature of Christ and God, some quite different from the orthodox consensus that arose. The content of revelation which included accounts of religious

[81] Alston, "Epistemic circularity," p. 17.

[82] See Kenneth Scott Latourette's *A History of Christianity*, New York: Harper and Row, 1975, pp. 140–145.

experience was a part of that, but religious experiences generally were not appealed to. Those doctrines were the product of discussion, debate, and sometimes compromise.

It is the consensus among New Testament scholars that the earliest Christians thought of themselves as Jews, bound by the Torah. They thought that Jesus was in fact the (fully human) promised Messiah and was raised from the dead and taken into heaven to return soon to usher in the world to come. Accounts of who and what Jesus was diversified over the following decades. The Ebionites, for example, thought that to be a Christian one must keep the law of Moses. They continued into at least the late second century. Some thought that Jesus was divine, and so he could not have been actually crucified; his physical body must have been a mere appearance. They were called Docetists, one kind of Gnostics.[83] The view that he was both fully divine and fully human won the day, but not decisively until the fourth century.

The canonical gospels themselves were written after some of that diversification had already taken place and may show in their diversity different developing ideas of God.[84] The Gospel of Mark, generally agreed to be the first Gospel to be written and distributed, presents Jesus as the Messiah, but there is no hint of him being divine. At his baptism, a voice from heaven says, "You are My beloved Son, in You I am well-pleased."[85] This clearly echoes Psalm 2:7, "You are my son; today I have begotten you," referring to King David, indicating that Jesus is chosen by God to rule, as David was.[86] Through the entire passion narrative, Jesus says almost nothing, until he cries out on the cross, "My God, My God, why have You forsaken Me?"[87] Compare that picture with Matthew and Luke, both later than and dependent on Mark, who give Jesus a miraculous birth narrative (two different ones, in fact), as if to say he must have been born special, and was not just an ordinary human chosen and elevated by God. He is born of a virgin, his birth is announced by the appearance of a star

[83] A brief discussion of the Ebionites, who denied the divinity of Christ, and the Gnostics (especially Valentinians and Marcionites) who denied the humanity of Christ can be found in Paul Johnson's *A History of Christianity*, New York: Atheneum, 1980, pp. 42–48.

[84] See for example Richard E. Rubenstein, *How Jesus Became God*, New York: Harper Collins, 1999; Bart Ehrman, *When Jesus Became God*; Paula Frederiksen, *From Jesus to Christ: The Origins of the New Testament Images of Jesus*, New Haven: Yale University Press, 1990; and *When Christians Were Jews: The First Generation*, New Haven: Yale University Press, 2008.

[85] Mark 1:11, New American Standard translation.

[86] Some early manuscripts actually have "this day I have begotten you," and it also so cited in several early sources. Bart Ehrman in *The Orthodox Corruption of Scripture: The Effect of Early Christological Controversies on the Text of the New Testament*, New York: Oxford University Press, 1993, p. 65, says this is reason to believe it is the original reading of Luke's gospel, which was later corrected by scribes to match the words of Mark and Matthew. This is a minority view among New Testament scholars, but is an intriguing possibility.

[87] Mark 15:34, New American Standard translation.

and by the announcement of angels, and important people come from far away to find and worship him. When he is crucified, he does not cry out in despair and Luke has him conversing with a thief who is crucified alongside him.[88] Still, they do not call him God, but rather the Son of God. John, the last Gospel to be written, is the only one of the four that unambiguously calls him God. The story does not begin with a miraculous birth, but with an eternally pre-existent Logos, who was present at and a party to the creation of the world. When it comes time for him to die, he behaves quite calmly, speaking to several people along the way. When he dies, he says "It is finished!"[89] He is not only special from birth, but from eternity past. He is and has always been God. It is telling that the controversies on these doctrines were settled more or less finally by ecumenical councils, in which church leaders discussed and decided what would count as orthodoxy.

This is an example from Christian doctrine, but the same story could be told about Judaism and Islam. Moses purportedly encountered God in a burning bush and received the Torah. Immediately, the people of Israel worked to interpret and apply it, and new doctrines developed. The culmination of this process is found in the Talmud and the general practice of Rabbinical discussion. Consider, for example, kashrut. The command "You are not to boil a young goat in the milk of its mother"[90] turns into a rule against eating meat and dairy at the same meal, and even to the need for separate utensils for meat and dairy. In the end, things are taken to be Jewish doctrine that are not stated anywhere in Torah and were certainly not revealed to Moses. Similarly, Muhammad purportedly talks to the angel Jibril and receives the revelation of the Qur'an, and what it says about prayer times and fasting rules gets elaborated by discussion of *hadith*,[91] and further elaborated by arguments from analogy and general consensus of the *umma*. Things become Islamic doctrine that are not explicitly in the Qur'an, and certainly were not revealed to Muhammad. The Christian story is a bit different because none of the founding experiences were direct revelations of doctrine except as direct evidence for the resurrection. The only cases in the New Testament in which other doctrines are revealed are Peter's vision of the clean and unclean animals[92] and possibly Paul's receiving the revelation of the gospel.[93] The books of the New Testament are thought by Christians to be

[88] Luke 23:39–43. [89] John 19:30, New American Standard translation.

[90] Exodus 23:19, New American Standard translation. The commandment is repeated twice more, in Exodus 34:26 and Deuteronomy 14:21. A nice discussion of the ins and outs of the development of this part of kashrut can be found in Kenneth Lasson's "Sacred Cows, Holy Wars: Exploring the Limits of Law in the Regulation of Raw Milk and Kosher Meat," *DePaul Business and Commercial Law Journal* 13 (2014), 1–66.

[91] Orally transmitted traditions about the life of the prophet Muhammad. [92] Acts 10:6–19.

[93] Galatians 1:11–12, New American Standard translation: "For I would have you know, brethren, that the gospel which was preached by me is not according to man. For I neither received it from man, nor was I taught it, but I received it through a revelation of Jesus Christ."

inspired by God, but none purport to be the direct words of God. Even the words of Jesus himself are only relayed to us by others who do not claim to be speaking for God.

This is the story of how religious doctrines come to be, at least for the religions whose origins we know. Some extraordinary individual or group of individuals have religious experiences that transform their view of the world. The Buddha sees the cause-and-effect nature at the bottom of all phenomena. Muhammad encounters the angel Jibril in a cave near Mecca. Moses encounters a burning bush in the desert. And Jesus' disciples encounter their teacher, who they thought was dead, resurrected and back among them. They tell others, who discuss what it means, elaborate on it, and pass it on. There can be, at this stage, disagreements about what it means and how to live in the light of it. Some of those who come later will have similar experiences, confirming their understanding of their new world view. Eventually, after a doctrinal orthodoxy is reached, experiences that differ from that consensus are dismissed as not veridical. Religious experiences are crucial to the beginnings, but we must not overestimate their contribution to resulting bodies of doctrine and practice.

In particular, the monotheistic religions of today seem to insist on the idea of religious experience as the primary mode of knowledge of God. In particular, they insist on the idea that God wishes to be in an ongoing relationship with human beings. Though not everyone can be a prophet, everyone can be in touch with God. This is a truly remarkable idea: that finite creatures can have experiential contact with the one true God, the ruler and creator of the universe, in all his infinite transcendence. The transcendence of the Almighty poses various difficulties for finite minds, including the inadequacy of our human concepts to capture his true nature, but perhaps the most troubling is how a mere mortal could experience the reality of such a being in such a way as to derive meaningful information.

One might get the impression from the previous discussion that religious experience has a vanishingly small role to play in the grounds of belief. It seems to contribute very little to the detailed content of religious belief. To draw that conclusion would be a mistake. Consider a person's belief system as a tree-like structure, the roots of which are the deliverances of experience, and the rest as the beliefs derived from them.[94] It is true that the roots are few, and the tree is vast. But roots can be few and nevertheless bear a lot of weight. In particular, religious experience's impact on the importance of the believer's doxastic commitments is enormous. This impact comes from the richness of the system it props up, whichever theological system that may be. The content of the beliefs

[94] This picture of a person's doxastic structure is just a simplifying picture to make a point and should not be taken as a necessary commitment for anything that follows.

in that system are themselves items of great importance to the believer, and so they have great value for the believer. Beyond that, they underlie commitments *about* values that the believer holds and organizes her life around.

> "Do not be afraid, then, if He is pleased to speak with you, for He does this for the greater good of those who love Him. His love for those to whom He is dear is by no means so weak. He shows it in every way possible. Why then, my sisters, do we not show Him love in so far as we can? Consider what a wonderful exchange it is if we give Him our love and receive His." – St. Teresa of Avila, *The Way of Perfection*

Bibliography

Alston, William P. "Epistemic Circularity," *Philosophy and Phenomenological Research* 47 (1986), 319–349.

Reprinted in *Epistemic Justification: Essays in the Theory of Knowledge*, Ithaca: Cornell University Press, 1989, pp. 319–349.

Perceiving God: The Epistemology of Religious Experience, Ithaca: Cornell University Press, 1991.

Axtell, Guy. *Problems of Religious Luck: Assessing the Limits of Reasonable Religious Disagreement*, Lanham: Lexington Books/Rowman & Littlefield, 2019.

Barrett, J. L. "Exploring the Natural Foundations of Religion," *Trends in Cognitive Sciences* 4 (2000), 29–34.

Boyer, Pascal. *Religion Explained: The Evolutionary Origins of Religious Thought*, New York: Basic Books, 2001.

Byrne, Alex. "Inverted Qualia," *The Stanford Encyclopedia of Philosophy* (Winter Ed.), Edward N. Zalta (ed.), 2018, https://plato.stanford.edu/archives/win2018/entries/qualia-inverted/.

Byrne, Rhonda. *The Secret*, New York: Simon and Schuster, 1994.

Catechism of the Catholic Church. Vatican City: Libreria Editrice Vaticana, 1993.

Clarke, Arthur C. *Profiles of the Future: An Inquiry into the Limits of the Possible*, New York: Harper & Row, 1973.

Coady, Cecil A. J. *Testimony: A Philosophical Study*, New York: Clarendon Press, 1992.

DuBois, Page. *A Million and One Gods: The Persistence of Polytheism*, Cambridge: Harvard University Press, 2014.

Dretske, Fred. *Seeing and Knowing*, Chicago: The University of Chicago Press, 1969.

Duncan, Ronald *Selected Writings of Mahatma Gandhi*, Boston: The Beacon Press, 1951.

Ehrman, Bart. *The Orthodox Corruption of Scripture: The Effect of Early Christological Controversies on the Text of the New Testament*, New York: Oxford University Press, 1993.

How Jesus Became God: The Exaltation of a Jewish Preacher from Galilee, New York: Harper One, 2014.

Ekstrom, Laura W. "Suffering as Religious Experience," in Peter Van Inwagen (ed.), *Christian Faith and the Problem of Evil*, Grand Rapids: Eerdmans Press, 2004, pp. 95–110.

Findlay, John N. "Can God's Existence Be Disproved?" *Mind*, 57, 226 (1948), 176–183. *JSTOR*, www.jstor.org/stable/2250690.

Frederiksen, Paula. *From Jesus to Christ: The Origins of the New Testament Images of Jesus*, New Haven: Yale University Press, 1990.

When Christians Were Jews: The First Generation, New Haven: Yale University Press, 2008.

Gale, Richard M. "Swinburne's Argument from Religious Experience," in Alan G. Padgett (ed.), *Reason and the Christian Religion*, New York: Clarendon Press, 1994, pp. 39–63.

Gelfert, Axel. *A Critical Introduction to Testimony*, New York: Bloomsbury Academic, 2014.

Gowans, Christopher, *Philosophy of the Buddha*, New York: Routledge, 2003.

Hempel, Carl Gustav. "Reduction: Ontological and Linguistic Facets," in S. Morgenbesser, P. Suppes, & M. White (eds.), *Philosophy, Science, and Method: Essays in Honor of Ernest Nagel*, New York: St. Martin's Press, 1969, pp. 179–199.

Hick, John. *An Interpretation of Religion: Human Responses to the Transcendent*, 2nd ed. New Haven: Yale University Press, 2004 (1989).

Hoffmeier, James K. *Akhenaten and the Origin of Monotheism*, New York: Oxford, 2015.

Howard-Snyder, Daniel. "Who or What Is God, According to John Hick?" *Topoi* 36 (2017), 571–586.

Jackson, Frank, "Epiphenomenal Qualia," *Philosophical Quarterly* 32 (1982), 127–136.

James, William. *The Varieties of Religious Experience: A Study in Human Nature Being the Gifford Lectures on Natural Religion Delivered at Edinburgh in 1901–1902*, New York: Longmans, Green, 1917.

"The Will to Believe," in Alburey Castell (ed.), *Essays in Pragmatism*, New York: Hafner Press, 1948, p. 88–109.

Johnson, Paul. *A History of Christianity*, New York: Atheneum, 1980.

Lasson, Kenneth. "Sacred Cows, Holy Wars: Exploring the Limits of Law in the Regulation of Raw Milk and Kosher Meat," *DePaul Business and Commercial Law Journal* 13 (2014), 1–66.

Latourette, Kenneth Scott. *A History of Christianity*, New York: Harper and Row, 1975, pp. 140–145.

Laumakis, Stephen J., *An Introduction to Buddhist Philosophy*, Cambridge: Cambridge University Press, 2008.

Lewis, Clive S. *The Abolition of Man*, London: Oxford University Press, 1943.

James P. Mallory, & Adams, Douglas Q. (2006). *The Oxford Introduction to Proto-Indo-European and the Proto-Indo-European World*. Chapter 23, "Religion," New York: Oxford University Press.

My Jewish Learning, "The Shema: How Listening Leads to Oneness," www.myjewishlearning.com/article/the-shema-how-listening-leads-to-oneness/ Accessed 1/25/2023.

Oord, Thomas J. "Experiencing God in Nature." April 3, 2019, https://thomasjayoord.com/index.php/blog/archives/experiencing-god-in-nature#_edn2. Accessed 1/27/2023.

Otto, Rudoph. *The Idea of the Holy*, New York: Oxford, 1950.

Pagels, Elaine. *Adam, Eve and the Serpent: Sex and Politics in Early Christianity*, New York: Vintage Books, 1989.

The Origin of Satan: How Christians Demonized Jews, Pagans, and Heretics, New York: Vintage Books, 1995.

Pike, Nelson. "Omnipotence and God's Ability to Sin," *American Philosophical Quarterly*, 6, 3(1969), 208–216. *JSTOR*, www.jstor.org/stable/20009309.

Plantinga, Alvin. *Warranted Christian Belief*, New York: Oxford University Press, 2000. *ProQuest Ebook Central*, https://ebookcentral.proquest.com/lib/ttu/detail.action?docID=3052388. Accessed 1/25/2023.

Rachels, James. "God and Human Attitudes," *Religious Studies* 7 (1971), pp. 325–337.

Rubenstein, Richard E. *How Jesus Became* God, New York: Harper Collins, 1999.

Russell, Jeffrey Burton. *Satan: The Early Christian Tradition*, Ithaca: Cornell University Press, 1987.

Sayre-McCord, Geoff, "Metaethics," *The Stanford Encyclopedia of Philosophy* (Summer Ed.), Edward N. Zalta (ed.), 2014, https://plato.stanford.edu/archives/sum2014/entries/metaethics/.

Schellenberg, John L. *The Hiddenness Argument*, New York: Oxford University Press, 2015.

Schleiermacher, Friedrich. *On Religion: Speeches to Its Cultured Despisers*, Richard Crouter (trans. & ed.), Cambridge: Cambridge University Press, 1988.

Stark, Rodney. *One True God*, Princeton: Princeton University Press, 2001.

Stump, Eleonore. *Wandering in Darkness: Narrative and the Problem of Suffering*, New York: Oxford University Press, 2010.

Swinburne, Richard. *Coherence of Theism*. New York: Oxford University Press, 1977. *ProQuest Ebook Central*, https://ebookcentral.proquest.com/lib/ttu/detail.action?docID=3053289. Accessed 1/25/2023.

"Could There Be More than One God?" *Faith and Philosophy* 5 (1988), 225–241.

Teresa of Avila. *The Way of Perfection*. E. Alison Peers, trans., New York: Image Books, 1964.

Thanissaro, Bikkhu trans. "Chiggala Sutta: The Hole" (SN 56.48), *Access to Insight (BCBS Ed.)*, July 1, 2010, www.accesstoinsight.org/tipitaka/sn/sn56/sn56.048.than.html.

Wainwright, William. "Monotheism", *The Stanford Encyclopedia of Philosophy* (Fall Ed.), Edward N. Zalta (ed.), 2018, https://plato.stanford.edu/archives/fall2018/entries/monotheism/.

"Jonathan Edwards and the Hiddenness of God," in Daniel Howard-Snyder, & Paul K. Moser (eds.), *Divine Hiddenness: New Essays*, New York: Cambridge University Press, 2002, pp. 98–119.

Webb, Mark Owen, "Religious Experience as Doubt Resolution," *International Journal for Philosophy of Religion* 18 (1985), 81–86.

"An Eliminativist Theory of Religion," *Sophia* 48 (2009), 35–42.

"Meaning and Value in Religious Experience," in the Paul Moser, & Chad Meister (eds.), *Cambridge Companion to Religious Experience*, New York: Cambridge University Press, 2020.

"Religious Experience", *The Stanford Encyclopedia of Philosophy* (Fall Ed.), Edward N. Zalta, & Uri Nodelman (eds.), 2022, https://plato.stanford.edu/archives/fall2022/entries/religious-experience/.

Wellhausen, Julius. Jay Sutherland Black and Allan Menzies, trans. *Prolegomena to the History of Ancient Israel, with a reprint of the article "Israel" from the Encyclopedia Brittanica*, New York: World, 1957.

Wharton, Edward C. *Christianity: A Clear Case of History*. West Monroe: Howard, 1977.

Yandell, Keith, *Epistemology of Religious Experience*, Cambridge: Cambridge University Press, 1993.

Zangwill, Nick. "The Myth of Religious Experience," *Religious Studies* 40, 1 (March, 2004) 1–22.

Dedicated to my first philosophical mentors:
Ed Averill, Danny Nathan, and Howard Curzer.
They taught me how to be a philosopher, a teacher, and a mensch.

Cambridge Elements

Religion and Monotheism

Paul K. Moser

Loyola University Chicago

Paul K. Moser is Professor of Philosophy at Loyola University Chicago. He is the author of *God in Moral Experience; Paul's Gospel of Divine Self-Sacrifice; The Divine Goodness of Jesus; Divine Guidance; Understanding Religious Experience; The God Relationship; The Elusive God* (winner of national book award from the Jesuit Honor Society); *The Evidence for God; The Severity of God; Knowledge and Evidence* (all Cambridge University Press); and *Philosophy after Objectivity* (Oxford University Press); coauthor of *Theory of Knowledge* (Oxford University Press); editor of *Jesus and Philosophy* (Cambridge University Press) and *The Oxford Handbook of Epistemology* (Oxford University Press); and coeditor of *The Wisdom of the Christian Faith* (Cambridge University Press). He is the coeditor with Chad Meister of the book series *Cambridge Studies in Religion, Philosophy, and Society.*

Chad Meister

Affiliate Scholar, Ansari Institute for Global Engagement with Religion, University of Notre Dame

Chad Meister is Affiliate Scholar at the Ansari Institute for Global Engagement with Religion at the University of Notre Dame. His authored and co-authored books include *Evil: A Guide for the Perplexed* (Bloomsbury Academic, 2nd edition); *Introducing Philosophy of Religion* (Routledge); *Introducing Christian Thought* (Routledge, 2nd edition); and *Contemporary Philosophical Theology* (Routledge). He has edited or co-edited the following: *The Oxford Handbook of Religious Diversity* (Oxford University Press); *Debating Christian Theism* (Oxford University Press); with Paul Moser, *The Cambridge Companion to the Problem of Evil* (Cambridge University Press); and with Charles Taliaferro, *The History of Evil* (Routledge, in six volumes). He is the co-editor with Paul Moser of the book series *Cambridge Studies in Religion, Philosophy, and Society.*

About the Series

This Cambridge Element series publishes original concise volumes on monotheism and its significance. Monotheism has occupied inquirers since the time of the Biblical patriarch, and it continues to attract interdisciplinary academic work today. Engaging, current, and concise, the Elements benefit teachers, researched, and advanced students in religious studies, Biblical studies, theology, philosophy of religion, and related fields.

Cambridge Elements

Religion and Monotheism

Elements in the Series

Monotheism and Narrative Development of the Divine Character in the Hebrew Bible
Mark McEntire

God and Being
Nathan Lyons

Monotheism and Divine Aggression
Collin Cornell

Jewish Monotheism and Slavery
Catherine Hezser

Open Theism
Alan R. Rhoda

African Philosophy of Religion and Western Monotheism
Kirk Lougheed, Motsamai Molefe and Thaddeus Metz

Monotheism and Pluralism
Rachel S. Mikva

The Abrahamic Vernacular
Rebecca Scharbach Wollenberg

Monotheism and Fundamentalism: Prevalence, Potential, and Resilience
Rik Peels

Emotions and Monotheism
John Corrigan

Monotheism and Peacebuilding
John D Brewer

Monotheism and Religious Experience
Mark Owen Webb

A full series listing is available at: www.cambridge.org/er&m

For EU product safety concerns, contact us at Calle de José Abascal, 56–1°, 28003 Madrid, Spain or eugpsr@cambridge.org.

www.ingramcontent.com/pod-product-compliance
Ingram Content Group UK Ltd.
Pitfield, Milton Keynes, MK11 3LW, UK
UKHW022143080726
473066UK00010B/718

* 9 7 8 1 1 0 8 9 5 8 0 2 8 *